Developing
Early Literacy Skills

Developing
Early Literacy Skills

Practical Ideas & Activities

Katharine Bodle

Please note that the term 'school' is used in this book to denote primary school, pre-school, infant school, nursery or playgroup.

For readers outside the UK, the age ranges for the classes mentioned are as follows: Reception: 4–5 years, Year 1: 5–6 years and Year 2: 6–7 years

Note also that, for the sake of clarity alone, the masculine pronoun 'he' is used in the activity descriptions to refer to the individual child.

First published in 2006 by
Speechmark Publishing Ltd, 6–8 Oxford Court, St James Road, Brackley, NN13 7XY, UK
info@speechmark.net
www.speechmark.net

002-5336/Printed in the United Kingdom/1010

British Library Cataloguing in Publication Data
Bodle, Katharine
    Early Literacy Skills
    1. Language arts (Early childhood) 2. Language arts (Elementary) 3. Early childhood education – Activity programs 4. Education, Elementary – Activity programs
    I. Title
    372.6'044

ISBN-13: 978 0 86388 538 9
ISBN-10: 0 86388 538 1

Contents

Acknowledgements

With grateful thanks to those inspirational colleagues and children I have worked with. Thanks also to my family for their constant support.

Dedicated to my children, with all my love.

Introduction

The ideas and activities in this manual were developed from good classroom practice, and from techniques used by a teacher of dyslexic learners to help older children with specific learning difficulties. The activities have subsequently been used with children in mainstream education and children with special educational needs in whole-class, group and individual situations. (Symbols show which activities are suitable for group or class participation.)

The activities in this book can be (and have been) used by parents at home and by teachers, LSAs and nursery nurses in primary school, pre-school and early years settings. Please note that, for clarity, these settings are referred to here by the general term *school*.

Key facts

The key facts below put *Developing Early Literacy Skills* in context, outlining who will find it useful and why. Use this section to answer your initial questions.

Why is early literacy important?
Early literacy skills are important because they form the foundation on which children must build if they are to become competent readers and writers. Some children acquire literacy skills with ease; others need a structured approach to learning, with skills built gradually and cumulatively.

What does this manual do?
This manual provides a framework of specific activities for use with children who are showing early signs of literacy-based specific learning difficulties. These activities will also benefit the older child who lacks a foundation of early literacy skills, either as a result of inappropriate teaching, or because he has a specific learning difficulty.

Who is this manual for?

Developing Early Literacy Skills is aimed at teachers, learning support assistants (LSAs), nursery nurses and other professionals who are working with pre-school children or older children with literacy difficulties. Some of the activities provided are also suitable for parents and carers to carry out with children at home in consultation with these professionals.

Who should I consult for further assistance?

Professionals, parents and carers who suspect that the child they are working with has a specific learning difficulty such as dyslexia should consult an appropriate specialist. Who to contact will differ depending on the needs of the child, but could include the school SEN coordinator (SENCO), a speech therapist, educational psychologist or specialist dyslexia teacher.

Would ICT materials help the children I am working with?

ICT can play an important part in a child's learning at an early stage as it involves auditory, visual and kinaesthetic (multi-sensory) learning. Its immediacy and fast feedback and 'rewards' can also provide extra motivation for many children with literacy difficulties. Some ICT resources and suppliers are included in the resources list at the back of this book (see p150).

How to use this manual

The manual is divided into six sections. Section 1 provides activities that will help ensure that children have the basic skills and behaviours that are essential for them to work on the skills presented in the other sections. Sections 2 to 6 cover the chronological development of skills which an 'average' pre-school child will acquire before and during his first year in school. However, as these skills interrelate, activities from different sections can be used simultaneously, depending on the needs of the child or group.

Section 1: Basic skills

The aim of this section is to help children develop the basic skills that they need to take full advantage of the activities provided in the rest of the book. Many of these skills are general and do not necessarily relate directly to literacy.

The basic skills covered are:
- using spoken language
- sharing reading
- turn-taking
- being aware of sounds
- using auditory and visual memory
- sequencing.

Section 2: Rhyming

Poems and rhyming games give children a firm foundation for later spelling work. However, children with specific learning difficulties may find rhyme very difficult and the activities in this section are tailored to the needs of this group in particular. As well as explaining how nursery songs and rhymes may be used to the full, this part of the book provides specific activities on identifying and generating rhymes.

Section 3: Learning the alphabet

Learning the alphabet and then learning how it represents different sounds are essential components of competent reading and spelling. This section focuses specifically on the alphabet, looking first at how you might assess the child's current knowledge, then providing activities that will help him to develop this knowledge further. A lively selection of alphabet and letter identification games are provided, together with a checklist that will help you keep a record of the child's progress.

Section 4: Phonological awareness

Children need to understand that speech is made up of words, which can be further broken down into sounds. They also need to learn that these sounds are linked to letters and letter strings. This association is commonly referred to as phonics, and the term is also used to describe a particular method for teaching reading. Moving on from the rhyme activities in section 2 and the alphabet activities in section 3, this part of the book brings sounds and letters together with a series of activities on syllables and on sound identification. The technicalities of identifying different speech sounds are described in an accessible way, and useful resources are provided.

Section 5: Reading

The introduction to this section describes the four key methods of teaching reading and suggests how they may best be combined within an environment that encourages children to respect and enjoy books to the full. The activities provided will help you to share books with children, enabling them to identify the different parts of books and even to make their own. As the section progresses, the child is required to look increasingly closely at words and the letter sounds within them. The section concludes with a Reading Pack routine which will help to consolidate the child's learning.

Section 6: Writing and handwriting

After a thorough introduction which covers both why writing is important and the earliest stages in the development of writing skills, this section provides a wide range of activities. The first group of activities help to develop the child's fine motor skills. Once these are secure, patterning exercises are introduced, followed by specific handwriting activities. Useful copy masters are provided, giving you a range of ready-made tracing sheets that children will enjoy using.

Reference materials

At the back of the book you will find various useful lists of resources, suppliers, organisations that may be able to help you, and other publications. As mentioned earlier, some ICT resources and suppliers are included in the resources list.

Section structure

Each main section of the manual is structured in a similar way, as follows:

- Contents and list of activities
- Introduction and frequently asked questions
- Teaching guidelines
- Activities
- Photocopiable resource sheets.

Contents and list of activities

Every section has its own Contents page, so that you can find what you need quickly. It is followed by a full list of all the specific activities contained within the section, together with a note of the relevant photocopiable resource sheets.

Introduction and frequently asked questions

The introduction explains the importance of the particular skill in daily life and how a child might be encouraged to develop that skill. Any theoretical background is briefly explained, drawing out the practical implications for you as you work with the children in your care. Finally, some common questions that you may have are answered, giving you all the information you will need.

Teaching guidelines

Guidelines on the best approach for teaching this skill to children who have difficulties with literacy are offered. There is also an at-a-glance list of key points to remember. The checklist at the start of the photocopiable resource sheets section will help you to keep a record of activities carried out and progress made with each child. Each sheet includes a sample entry as an example of the kinds of notes you might want to make.

Activities

A list of activities fronts each activities section. The skill areas are sometimes covered in different ways. There are general activities – daily routines that will help the child to develop his literacy skills, and more specific (numbered) activities.

Activities are also designated as being suitable for school use, home use, or both. Please see page xii for further information and a fuller description of how to use the activities.

Photocopiable resource sheets

These sheets support both the general and more specific activities within the section. Instructions for use are provided either on the sheet itself, or in the instructions for the activity where it is used, as appropriate. They are suitable for use by teachers, LSAs and nursery nurses, as well as parents or carers, if appropriate: see the section on selecting activities, below (page xii).

How to use the activities

The activities within sections 2 to 6 follow a child's developmental order. Selection of activities will depend on your professional judgement and on the feedback you have obtained from the child's parents or carers.

Materials

The materials needed for each activity are listed beside the heading 'you will need'. Items include standard school equipment, everyday objects, toys which are readily available, items to be constructed from readily available materials and occasionally some commercial products. The list of materials is for guidance only; you can substitute them with other items if you feel that they are more appropriate or if availability is a problem. Where example materials have been provided as photocopiable resource sheets, such as rhyming pictures, they can often be extended using other published materials and games. When you ask parents or carers to try activities at home, it is important to ensure that they have the right equipment. Further information on materials that you can buy is given in 'Resources and suppliers', at the back of this manual (p150).

Variations and extensions

Variations are included with some activities. These give you ideas for similar activities and suggestions on how to vary them. This enables repetition and over-learning (repeating the same thing in a variety of ways) which is very important for those children with weak literacy skills. It is also important to ensure children remain stimulated to keep their interest.

Symbols

All of the activities are suitable to use with individual children. The symbol ᴴ is used to denote games which are also suitable for groups. Some activities can be used with a whole class if the teacher feels it is appropriate. These are indicated with the symbol ✳.

Activities for school

Please note: the term school can include primary school, pre-school, nursery or playgroup. When selecting activities for school use, consider:

- the willingness of the child to work in that setting with the designated adult
- the child's interests

- the availability of materials
- the school's ability to provide one-to-one or group activities in a quiet area.

Activities for home

These provide practical advice on using situations and materials readily available at home. They include using children's everyday routines and activities to develop the child's early literacy skills. These activities are generally for one-to-one work with a parent, family member or carer. However there are some instances in which other siblings or friends could be incorporated into the activity. When selecting activities for the parent and child to do at home, consider:

- The willingness of the child to work with the parent or carer
- The child's interests
- The availability of materials
- The social and cultural environment.

Activities at home should reinforce concepts and activities previously addressed in school. This should ensure the parent is not expected to teach. It is important that the activities are fun and are not stressful for either parent or child. They will be most beneficial if you can demonstrate and discuss them with parents and carers (where applicable), as well as providing them with the relevant resource sheet.

Checklists

Checklists are included at the start of each Resources section and are a means of recording the activities undertaken and the child's responses to them. A completed example is provided for guidance at the top of each checklist.

Setting up teaching situations in school

The teaching environment

Bear in mind the following points before you begin your session, whatever the setting.

1 Choose a quiet area.
2 Sit the child opposite you whenever possible.
3 Remove clutter from the workspace.
4 Ensure all your materials are to hand.
5 Seat the child appropriately with desk and chair at the correct height.

Grouping and seating

1 Seat groups in a semi-circle where possible. If you sit at the front opposite the group, this will give everyone a good view both of you and of the materials. With this arrangement you should clearly see every child's responses.
2 Seat active children between more passive children and ensure that those at the centre of the semi-circle do not dominate the activity to the detriment of those at the edge.
3 When seating children on the floor, consider laying down carpet tiles so that they have a 'base' to sit on; this way the semi-circle shape can be maintained.

Planning and carrying out the activities

1 Choose activities appropriate to the child's needs, and to his intellectual and concentration levels.
2 Build on prior knowledge whenever possible; refer back to previous activities the child has undertaken.
3 Be clear about your aims and objectives for the activity. Refer to the checklists from previous sessions.
4 Be clear as to how long the activity will take. Short sessions of around 10 minutes per activity are usually long enough. This may need to be adapted depending on the child's concentration span.
5 Use clear instructions and limit them to a maximum of three at a time.
6 Where possible enable the child to discover for himself what it is you want him to learn. You will need to guide the child using questioning and suggestion, but if he discovers the answer for himself he is more likely to remember it.

7 Show the child how to respond by giving him an example of an acceptable response; this is known as modelling. Modelling is one of the most powerful techniques available for encouraging children to learn.

8 Be aware that the activities may need to be undertaken several times before the child is secure with a concept.

9 Be flexible.

10 Be positive – always.

Tips for working with children at home

Patience
Be patient and positive. Children learn at different rates. Some children will find the activities in this book harder than others; some will be keener to work with their parents than others. All children have times when they do not want to cooperate.

Timing
1 Choose a time to work with the child that suits you both. It is difficult to work with a child who is tired or hungry.

2 Make sure that the time you choose is free from other distractions.

3 A routine is useful: for example, regularly playing a game after supper, before bedtime or straight after breakfast.

4 Pick a time when you are both mentally alert and relaxed.

5 Keep sessions short. The most beneficial sessions usually last between 10 and 15 minutes.

Environment
1 Choose a quiet, tidy room where you will not be disturbed. Ensure that the child's siblings are either meaningfully occupied or asleep.

2 If you have to share a room with other members of the family you should clear any toys or other items off the floor or table.

3 Cover patterned work surfaces with a plain piece of paper or a tablecloth to minimise visual distractions.

4 Ensure that you are able to be at the same level so that you can make eye contact easily without looking down at your child.

5 Turn off the television, radio or CD player.

6 Make sure that the child is comfortable. Some children find sitting on the floor or a hard chair very difficult; cushions can help, but do not use them if they too prove to be a distraction.

Be flexible

Follow the child's lead. If he has particular interests – such as transport, animals or food – then incorporate them where possible within the activities, even if you have to change an activity slightly.

Be positive

It is particularly important to be positive if a child finds something hard or makes a lot of mistakes.

1 Try to accentuate the positive at all times.
2 Help the child to identify his own mistakes.
3 Guide the child so that he discovers new things for himself rather than having everything pointed out.
4 Above all, give the child lots of praise so that he is keen to work with you on these activities again.

REMEMBER

1 Adopt a positive, multi-sensory approach.
2 Build on a child's previous success.
3 Ensure that the child does not feel any sense of failure.
4 Make learning fun.

SECTION **1**
Basic skills

Introduction

The activities in Sections 2 to 6 assume that children have the basic skills that one would normally expect of their age group. If these skills are weak or lacking, then take some time to work on them by using this section before you start the activities in the rest of the manual. This should ensure that each child derives maximum benefit from the activities and makes progress in improving his literacy skills.

Using spoken language

If you encourage children to use spoken language in its correct form, they will be more likely to use complex sentences containing rich and varied vocabulary when writing. Their comprehension when reading will also improve as they will have a wide knowledge of words to draw upon.

Sharing reading

Sharing rhymes, stories and other books will help children to extend their vocabulary and will open the door to a whole new world of entertainment and information.

Turn-taking

This is an important life skill, and many games and activities within schools rely on children being able to take turns. Turn-taking is also important in conversing with others, with questions and answers alternating between different people.

Being aware of sounds

Being aware of sounds in the environment ensures that a child has the ability to listen critically and distinguish sounds in the spoken word. This is necessary when breaking words down into individual sounds (*phonemes*) when reading or spelling.

Using auditory and visual memory

A good memory is important in all aspects of learning. The short-term or working memory can hold between five and nine items if trained properly; most people remember about seven items, and some can remember many more.

It is important to learn how to 'chunk' items together in order to remember them more effectively. For example, it would be difficult to remember *axpvswluqity*, but it is easier to remember even a nonsense word like *redbincastal*. This second 'word' has the same number of letters as the first, but we can chunk it into *red/bin/castal* and remember it as three items. It is possible to train the short-term memory and by doing this we enable information to be held longer, to be manipulated and to be placed in the long-term memory.

When working with children it is helpful to bear in mind that we all remember best those things that:

- we use or practise frequently
- we have learnt recently
- are important or meaningful to us.

Sequencing

Sequencing skills rely on memory and on seeing patterns. We use many sequences in our daily lives, from remembering the order in which to dress, to using the sequence of the alphabet (when using a telephone directory) or knowing the order of the days of the week (when planning ahead). This section contains activities and techniques that can be used to improve these basic skills. They can be used both to check whether the basics skills are in place and as reinforcement activities.

Teaching guidelines

1 Spend time listening to the child and observing him at play. This will enable you to assess which basic skills need further work.
2 Work through your choice of activities: most are suitable for one-to-one use or for work in pairs – unless otherwise indicated.
3 Be aware that some of these skills may take time to develop. The child may need to repeat the activities many times before his learning is consolidated. Therefore the activities must be adapted so that they do not become boring for the child.

Remember

1 Be positive.
2 Model appropriate behaviour and the language you are expecting so that the child can learn by example. For further information on modelling refer back to 'setting up teaching situations in school,' page xiv.
3 Many of these activities do not need to take place in organised sessions. Take opportunities for learning as they arise.

Using spoken language

General activities for school and home

When talking to young children it is important to use real words and to encourage a rich vocabulary. Reinforcing babyspeak will not be beneficial in the long run. If you do use babyspeak you should also reinforce the correct word by using it in context within the same sentence.

Modelling

Children learn best by modelling and so we should give them correct models to learn from. Children who muddle letters within words or words within sentences should not be explicitly corrected; instead, the adult should respond by modelling the sentence correctly.

> Child: 'Can I have bsgetti for tea?'
> Adult: 'Yes, of course you can have spaghetti for tea!'

As opposed to;

> Adult: 'It's not bsgetti – it's spaghetti'

Encourage children to use rich and varied vocabulary. This can be achieved by giving objects their correct label: a daffodil rather than a flower; a combine harvester rather than a tractor. It is also important to encourage children to use descriptive language whenever possible, without appearing too contrived.

> Child: 'Look at the bus'
> Adult: 'Yes, it is a big red bus isn't it? I wonder where it is going?'

Positive modelling will ensure that the child maintains good self-esteem rather than becoming reluctant to speak. Those children who attempt to use more complex vocabulary but are frequently corrected by an adult will soon revert to using more basic vocabulary. Sensitive, positive modelling should prevent regression of this kind.

Sharing reading

Children who have listened to stories and rhymes from infancy will have been exposed to a wealth of rich language and rhythm. They will also have learnt to sit and listen, to concentrate on pictures and on the sounds of language. All of these are useful skills that they will expand upon using the activities within this book.

General activities for home

Babies enjoy cloth books and board books. Those with simple pictures with definite images in bold colours are best. The experience of cuddling up to someone to share a book should be encouraged from a young age.

General activities for school and home

As babies become toddlers, tactile books and books with flaps or pop-ups encourage their concentration and interest. A range of books should be on offer, including:

- picture books with large, clear illustrations;
- books that include photographs of everyday objects and events;
- books that reflect a young child's experiences, such as starting at pre-school, going to visit grandparents or feeding the ducks.

Moving towards independent reading

As children move towards reading independently, make available a variety of books containing rhyme, repetition and interesting pictures. Pictures are very important because they encourage children to talk and can provide useful clues as to what may happen next in a story. Encourage children to join in with repetition and rhyme if possible. Your enthusiasm will help the child understand that books can be fun and exciting. Traditional tales are useful as they demonstrate particularly clearly that a story is carefully structured. As you read, use a different voice for each character. Remember to point to words as you read them. It is also important to show children how to look after books.

'Reading' from memory

It is absolutely fine for children to 'read' a book from memory and you should give praise and encouragement to a child who is able to do this. Whatever stage a child is at, it is important that you continue to read aloud to children and that it does not become a 'teaching activity'. Sharing a book on a one-to-one basis or in a group is important as it models reading skills. It also enables children to enjoy more complex stories than they could read themselves.

Turn-taking

General activities for school and home

Young children need to learn to take turns in a variety of situations. This is an important life skill; it is used, for example, when they take part in conversations, and when they play games with other children. Many children learn about turn-taking from an early age, through sharing toys with siblings and friends or through handing toys to adults and expecting them to hand them back.

When playing games, some children find turn-taking frustrating. You can help encourage cooperation by ensuring that the child understands the language involved. For example, when you say 'your turn', 'my turn' etc, accompany the instruction with a gesture – such as pointing to the appropriate person. Praise the child when he waits for his turn.

Turn-taking

Games that involve turn-taking include:

- rolling a ball to another person
- throwing a ball for another person to catch
- taking turns to pick a piece of fruit or crisps from a bowl
- being in charge of offering food to others in a group
- taking it in turns to play an instrument in pairs, then in a small group situation
- taking it in turns to use a piece of equipment, such as a sieve in the sand tray
- holding an object (such as a shell or pebble) when speaking during a conversation or sharing ideas in pairs or a group.

Being aware of sounds

Before a child can understand the idea that language and words are made up of sounds, a great deal of work on sounds is required. To help this process, some of the following activities may be tried. In addition you can draw attention to sounds within the environment, such as sounds made by the washing machine, birdsong, the wind or traffic.

Activities for school and home

Activity 1:
Locating sounds

Play this game using a blindfold, if the child is comfortable with this. Having blindfolded the child, you make a noise somewhere in the room, and invite the child to point to where they think the sound is coming from.

Activity 2:
Identifying sounds

Allow the child to identify objects by their sound alone – there are published lotto and tape games based on this idea (see Resources section). But you can also play this game with the objects around you at school or at home. Simply blindfold the child and then make noises using whatever is to hand. For example, in the kitchen you might put the toaster on, boil a kettle, run a tap, sweep the floor, open the fridge, or in the classroom you might sharpen a pencil, move a chair, draw with a crayon or open a door. Ask the child: 'What is this sound?'

Activity 3:
Sound shakers game

Ask the child to help you fill the containers with the objects, using only one type of object per container. Shake them and listen to the different sounds. Blindfold the child and shake the container. Ask the child: 'Which object is in the container?'

You will need:
five identical small containers with lids (the containers must be opaque); small items such as paperclips, lentils, sugar, a small bell and a ball of tin foil. Each one needs to fit in a container

Activity 4:
Distinguishing sounds

Find out whether the child can distinguish between loud and soft (or quiet) sounds. Being able to make this distinction will help the child when he is later asked to determine voiced and unvoiced sounds and also to locate stresses within words and syllables.

Using auditory and visual memory

Memory is important for language learning. It is possible to improve memory by using a range of fun-to-play games, and an improved memory will help greatly with organising and sequencing information.

Activities for school and home

Activity 5:
Kim's game

Lay a variety of objects on a tray. Allow the child time to look at the tray carefully. The tray is then removed or covered with a cloth. The child has to remember as many items on the tray as possible.

You will need:
a tray, 3–7 different objects, such as a ball, a spoon, a toy car, a model of an animal

Variation
An object is removed from the tray without the child seeing and the child has to name the object that has been removed.

Activity 6:
Sequencing pictures

Place a card face up and identify it. Then turn it over. If the child can remember it, place it face up again and add another card. Turn them over and continue until the child cannot remember any more. Repeat this activity using the same number of cards until you feel the child might be ready to add another.

You will need:
a set of pictures (these could be themed to appeal to the child's interest: for example, animals, transport, food etc)

Activtity 7:
Matching pairs

You will need:
picture pairs cards, such as those used for the game Snap

Choose around six pairs of pictures. Lay one card from each pair in a line and put the matching cards randomly next to the child. Ask the child to match the cards correctly by putting one of his cards on top of its matching partner in the line. This can also be done with socks when sorting out the laundry.

When this routine is established, place the pairs cards face down on the table and play a Pelmanism game. Take turns to turn over two cards with the aim of finding a pair. If a pair is found, the player keeps it and the player with the most pairs at the end wins.

Activity 8:
My Granny went shopping

You will need:
toy food or pictures of food and a basket

Put the food in a central location. Take turns to pick up the basket and say:

'My Granny went shopping and she bought _____ [for example, an apple].'

Pick up the apple and put it in the basket. Empty the basket and pass it to the next player. Each new player must repeat the previous player's shopping and add an object of their own. For example:

'My Granny went shopping and she bought _____ [an apple and a cake]'.

Continue until there are a maximum of seven items in the basket. At first you can accept the items in random order, but as the child becomes more proficient encourage him to repeat the items in order.

Variation
This game can also be played as a purely auditory activity – in the car, for example.

Activity 9
Can you do what I do?

Give a simple sequence of two instructions as you demonstrate an action. For example: 'Touch your nose, touch your toes'.

The child must copy the action in the correct sequence.

The adult can gradually build up to a more complex set of instructions. For example: 'Touch your nose, touch your toes, scratch your head, tickle your knee'

Variations
The adult can give the instructions orally or visually so the child has to either see and remember or hear and remember.

The adult can give random instructions, not building on those given previously.

The adult can pause between instructions then give the command 'Go!' when the child is to begin copying the sequence.

Activity 10:
Can you find it?

Ask the child to fetch items from across the room, starting with simple items. For example: 'Find me a pencil, a block and a counter'.

You will need:
a selection of objects such as coloured pencils, coloured large and small bricks, coloured counters, and coloured large and small beads

If the child follows your instructions correctly, ask for more items.

When the child is secure with this, increase the complexity of the instruction. For example: 'Find a red pencil, a large block and a blue bead'.

More items and different criteria (such as colour or size) can be used to extend the memory further.

Activity 11:
Sound pairs

Children take turns to shake a container and try to find its matching pair. This is an auditory version of a visual pairs Pelmanism game.

You will need:
10 identical small containers with lids (the containers must be opaque). These should be filled in pairs with small objects such as lentils, salt, a small bell, a marble, etc

Sequencing

Sequencing is something that children with specific learning difficulties find very difficult because of their poor auditory and visual memory. When playing with children it is important to model vocabulary linked to sequencing. For example: next, after, before, first, last. Regular practice with sequencing games and activities will be beneficial.

Activities for school and home

Activity 12:
Sequencing actions

The adult demonstrates an action, such as clapping hands. The child copies the action. The adult then repeats the first action and adds a second one: for example, clapping hands and then stamping one foot. Gradually introduce more actions until a sequence of six is achieved.

Activity 13:
Sequencing daily events

There are published picture cards available (for example, the ColorCards® series published by Speechmark) that sequence daily events such as getting up in the morning or cooking food. It is also possible to draw your own sequence cards, or even take a sequence of photographs. Discuss the pictures with the child in the correct order, then muddle them up and see if the child can sequence them correctly.

Variation
This activity could be extended. For example, use pictures that tell simple stories or show an animal's or an insect's lifecycle.

Activity 14:
Following a recipe

Cook something with the child, referring to the recipe to demonstrate that the sequence is important. Ask the child to tell you the next part of the sequence. Encourage them to think about why the sequence is necessary.

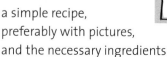

You will need:
a simple recipe, preferably with pictures, and the necessary ingredients

Activity 15:
Sequencing patterns

Create a pattern and discuss it with the child. Keep the pattern simple at first, involving perhaps only two colours. Verbalise the pattern again and ask the child to help find the next bead to make the pattern continue. As the child becomes more proficient, make the pattern more complex.

You will need:
coloured beads or cotton reels and string

Activity 16:
Visual timetable

Some children will enjoy following a visual timetable to show what is happening during the day. At the start of the day, discuss what is going to happen and select a card to represent each activity. The child should arrange the symbols in the correct order to show the sequence of the day. As each activity is completed, the symbol can be removed from the board.

You will need:
small cards with symbols on to represent the events of the day (Makaton® symbols can be useful for this, see Resources); a board to display them on

Activity 17:
Songs, rhymes and stories

There are many songs, stories and rhymes that use sequencing as their main theme. Examples include: 'Ten green bottles', 'There were ten in the bed', 'There was an old lady who swallowed a fly' and 'Five little ducks went swimming one day'. Sing, tell or recite these sequences until they become so familiar that the child is able to do so alone, whilst also understanding what the sequence means.

Resource Sheet 1.1: **Basic skills checklist**

Name _____   Class _____

Date	Activity	Comments
13/9	Visual memory: Kim's Game	Could remember 3 out of 5 items

SECTION 2
Rhyming

SECTION 2

Introduction

An ability to recognise and use rhyme is essential for later work on spelling. It is easy to spell *fat* if you can spell words such as *cat*, *mat* and *rat*. Being able to rhyme can take some of the pressure off learning each spelling as a separate entity.

Children with dyslexic tendencies can find rhyming very difficult. It is crucial that they develop listening skills, something that may not often be asked of them if they are constantly provided with visual images when hearing stories and rhymes. Traditional nursery rhymes may be regarded as old-fashioned; consequently, many children enter nursery and school without a sense of rhyme.

An easy way to foster a sense of rhyme in a child is to read plenty of poems and rhyming stories with him. There are many anthologies available; some suggestions are listed on *Resource sheet 2.14* at the end of this section. Otherwise a good bookshop or library should be able to help you choose from some of the best around. When reading to a child, he may begin to join in with the rhyme at the end of a sentence or page, especially if you hesitate and give him time to respond.

At the early stages of playing rhyming games, do not show the child the words on paper; instead, focus on their sounds. This means that you can use more complex words, too. However once a child has some knowledge of reading and spelling it is important only to use words that are also *spelt* with the same *rime* (that is, the end part of the word).

Please note that the words of some common nursery rhymes are supplied on *Resource sheets 2.2* and *2.3*.

Frequently asked questions

How can I help a child who always finds two words that begin with the same sound when asked to identify a rhyme?
You need to encourage the child to hear the end sounds of the word: at the moment he is stuck on the beginning (onset). To encourage this, over-emphasise the end part of the word (the rime) such as *cat, mat, rat.*

Should I use the term 'rhyme' or say 'sounds like' for younger children?
Sounds like is easier than the term rhyme for young children. However, if you use both words in conjunction, the child will soon understand the concept of rhyming and will be able to use the word rhyme correctly.

Teaching guidelines

1 Listen to the child reciting nursery rhymes (some examples are given on *Resource sheets 2.2* and *2.3*). Does he say the rhyme correctly?
2 Be aware that hearing rhyme does not come naturally to some children and a lot of overlearning must be carried out before they recognise it. For this reason, activities must be adapted so that they do not become boring for the child.
3 Having a pre-prepared list of rhyming words that you want to use can be helpful when undertaking these activities. Example lists are provided on *Resource sheets 2.4* and *2.5*. You might also consider collecting objects (or pictures of objects) with names that rhyme.

Remember

1 Be positive.
2 Model the activity for the child so he understands what is expected of him.
3 Take learning opportunities as they arise, both at home and in school.
4 Read rhyming poems and rhyming stories, and sing songs that rhyme as part of the child's general exposure to literature.
5 Use the Rhyming skills checklist (*Resource sheet 2.1*) to keep a record of the child's progress.

Learning nursery songs and rhymes

There are many books, CDs and DVDs of traditional nursery songs and rhymes available, as well as modern variations. A list of some of these is included on *Resource sheet 2.14*. The more exposure a child has to rhyme, the more chance he has of picking it up.

Activities for school

In group situations, ensure that the children know the rhymes and are not simply mumbling along with the crowd. This can be done by using the following activities.

Activity 18:
A line at a time

Choose a nursery rhyme. If you wish, you can use one of the rhymes on *Resource sheets 2.2* and *2.3*. Recite the rhyme together. Then recite it again: this time, you say the first line of the nursery rhyme and then point to a child to ask him to say the next line.

Variations
Start with a child saying the first line and passing an object to the next child to indicate that he must say the next line.

You take a turn and deliberately get the rhyme slightly wrong: see if the children notice!

Activity 19:
Tell us a rhyme

Ask two or three children to come forward and say a rhyme: this may help you to discover who knows the rhymes. However, if a child is reluctant to be singled out in this way, then it may be more appropriate to ask an adult helper to observe them during the session and feed back to you afterwards.

Activities at school for older children

Activity 20:
Act out a rhyme

Ask small groups of children to act out nursery rhymes to perform to others.

Variation
This can be done using mime and the audience has to guess which rhyme the children are performing.

Activity 21:
Extend a rhyme

Some nursery rhymes have more than one verse and children can rehearse these for performance.

Activity 22:
Change a rhyme

Identify the rhyming words within a traditional nursery rhyme.

Begin the nursery rhyme as normal but change one or two of the rhymes from the second line onwards. Pause before the rhyme ends so that the children can help find new words to make the rhyme work.

*'Jack and Jill went up the hill
To fetch a pail of jelly
Jack fell down and broke his crown
And Jill got very ... smelly.'*

*'Humpty Dumpty sat on a hill
Humpty Dumpty felt very ... ill
All the King's horses and all the King's sheep
Were found in the barn fast ... asleep.'*

These new class nursery rhymes can be displayed on a wall or in a book or may even be performed for others.

General activities for home

Make saying and singing rhymes part of daily routines such as car journeys or bedtime. Rhyming activities need no equipment when integrated into the child's daily routine: for example, singing 'Twinkle twinkle little star' at bedtime, or practising marching to 'The Grand Old Duke of York'. Include finger rhymes and games: try to choose those that rhyme. Well known rhymes and rhyming songs include:

- 'Jack and Jill'
- 'Humpty Dumpty'
- 'Miss Polly had a dolly'
- 'Little Miss Muffet'
- 'Mary, Mary, quite contrary'
- 'Dingle dangle scarecrow'
- 'Twinkle twinkle little star'
- 'Here is the church and here is the steeple'

The words for some further nursery rhymes are provided on *Resource sheets 2.2* and *2.3*.

Identifying rhymes

Activities for school

Activity 23:
Rhyme box

Place an object in a box: for example, a toy pig. Give rhyme clues for the child to guess the object, for example:

- 'It rhymes with dig.'
- 'The noise it makes rhymes with front.'
- 'The place where it lives rhymes with fly.'

You will need:
a box with a hole in the side, small toys and objects, a list of rhyming words *(see Resource sheets 2.4 and 2.5)*

Activity 24:
Rhyming bingo

The caller has the pack of rhyme cards. They will call out the first picture they pick up. If a player has a picture that rhymes with the word called, they place a counter on the rhyming picture on their board. The first one to cover all their pictures wins.

You will need:
1 rhyming bingo baseboard per player *(see Resource sheets 2.12 and 2.13)*, rhyming pairs cards and enough counters to complete all the sets of baseboards. Use the rhyme cards from *Resource sheets 2.6 to 2.10*

Activity 25:
Rhyming sets

Start with two sets of pictures. Identify them with the child. The child is asked to sort the pictures into sets that rhyme. For example: clock, lock, sock, block and pan, man, can, van.

You will need:
4 sets of pictures, each set including pictures of four objects whose names rhyme

Extension
Build up using all four sets of four pictures.

Extension for older children

Use word cards instead of pictures. If you use similar sounding and looking groups of words (such as words which rhyme with *ink* and words which rhyme with *mint*) then the children will need to look at each word closely to sort it.

Activity 26:
Tidy a rhyme

Seat the children in a circle. Hand out an object to each member of the group. Place a box in the centre of the circle. Say a word. All the children who have an object or picture that rhymes with that word holds them up. Go around the circle naming the objects. If the object rhymes the child places it in the box. Repeat with a different rhyme.

> **You will need:**
> objects or pictures of objects with simple rhymes

Extension for older children

This activity can be carried out with rhyming words written on cards.

Activities for school and home

Activity 27:
Odd one out

Say three words to the child and ask him to identify the one that does not rhyme, and is therefore the odd one out. For example:

Adult: 'Pig, cow, dig.'
Child: 'Cow is the odd one out.'

Extension

This activity can be extended by using four to six words instead of three.

SECTION 2

Activity 28:
Rhyming pairs

Initially use six or eight pairs of cards and turn them face up on a table. Identify with the players the names of the objects pictured. Pick a card and ask the child to pick another showing an object whose name rhymes with it: you may need to verbalise some of the object names again to reinforce the rhyme. Eventually you should be able to ask the children to give you pairs that sound the same. You can introduce more and more pairs at this point.

You will need:
rhyming pairs cards as provided on *Resource sheets 2.6* to *2.10*; if you wish to make your own cards, please see the lists of rhyming words on *Resource sheets 2.4* and *2.5*

Extension
To extend this, turn the cards over and play a Pelmanism game, where players take turns to pick a card and find its pair. Each player who finds a pair keeps it to one side and the player with the most pairs at the end is the winner.

Activity 29:
Rhyming Snap

Shuffle the cards and deal all the cards among the players so that each has the same number. Players place their cards in a pile, face down in front of them. They then take it in turns to turn up the top card on their own pile and place it face up in the centre, making a new pile. When a turned-up card rhymes with the one immediately beneath it, 'SNAP!' must be shouted. The first player to shout 'Snap!' then takes the central pile and puts it under their own pile. The last player left in the game is the winner.

You will need:
a set of rhyming pairs cards as provided on *Resource sheets 2.6* to *2.10*. Photocopy the sheets, glue them onto card and then cut them up

Activity 30:
Rhyme quiz

Ask the child questions about rhyme; for example:

- 'Black and sack, do they rhyme?'
- 'Flower and sour, do they rhyme?'
- 'Frog and duck, do they rhyme?'

You can even use nonsense words and children love to generate their own nonsense word rhymes.

- 'Simp and fimp, do they rhyme?'
- 'Freg and pluff, do they rhyme?'

This can progress to more complex questions:

- 'I am thinking of a word that rhymes with pink – is it sick or sink?'
- 'Can you tell me a word that rhymes with thin?'

As the questions become more open ended, the child will have to draw increasingly on his understanding of rhyme and you can therefore assess his rhyming ability.

Activity 31:
Rhyming riddles

Start by saying 'I am thinking of a word. What can it be?' and add questions, such as:

- 'It's something that smells nice and rhymes with sour. What is it?'
- 'It's somewhere that you live, that rhymes with mouse. What is it?'
- 'It's something that quacks and rhymes with truck. What is it?'
- 'It's something that a hen lays for you to eat and it rhymes with leg what is it?'

Activity 32:
Rhyming scrapbook

Collect pictures of objects whose names rhyme and, with the children, stick them into a book, one page per rhyme. Challenge the children to work out which is the most common or most unusual rhyme.

You will need:
pictures of objects that rhyme, glue, scrapbook

Activity 33:
Rhyming chain game

This game can be played by a child independently. However, it is useful if you are there at first to verbalise the rhyme with the child. (The first and last images – 'chain' and 'tick' – do not rhyme.) Place the cards with the green dots face up. Start with the chain and turn it over, find the card that rhymes with cat and turn it over. Keep going until the tick is face up.

You will need:
rhyming chain game (*see Resource sheets 2.11A and 2.11B*), made up according to the instructions on *Resource sheet 2.11A*

Extension for older children
Chain games are easy to make. They can be extended by using words and pictures.

The chain starts and is turned to reveal a word, the picture for that word is then found and turned to find the next word. Choose words where the rhyme is spelt the same at first then progress to words which are spelt differently: for example, begin with pea, sea, grin, thin, rake, cake, etc; then progress to pictures such as bread, shed, bear, chair.

Chain games may also be used with sound families of words to help with reading for example: peach, seat, leaf, bean, sheep, reel, tree, three, chief, thief, etc.

Generating rhymes

Activities for school and home

Activity 34:
Rhyming names

There are some songs, for example 'The Quartermaster's Stores' (*Ta-ra-ra Boom-de-ay: Songs for everyone*, see Resources list, p152), a traditional camp fire song, which incorporate names and their rhymes and can be adapted to include children's names. However, it is easy to make up your own sentences incorporating your child's name and a rhyme such as:

- 'Here comes Jack with a sack on his back.'
- 'Here comes Kate, she is always late.'

Names could include those of classmates or family members. Young children will find this very funny, even if they cannot create their own sentences without help. Just be careful not to offend anyone.

Activity 35:
I spy a rhyme

This game is based on the traditional 'I spy' game that many parents play with their children. In this variation, the name of the target object rhymes with the word given. This can take some children a little while to get used to. It goes like this:

'I spy with my little eye
Something that rhymes with …'

If the object is not visible then use the following:

'I hear with my little ear
Something that rhymes with …'

As the adult you need to ensure that you think of words with simple rhymes!

Activity 36:

Rhyming pictures

Create a picture around a rhyming sentence such as:

- 'Ten hens in pens'
- 'A big pig in a wig'
- 'A man with a pan in a can'

You will need:
drawing materials, glue, pictures from magazines

This can be done in a simple drawing or by getting a group of children to create different pictures. For example, pictures of a cat, a hat and a bat might be put on a picture of a mat.

Activity 37:

Silly nursery rhymes

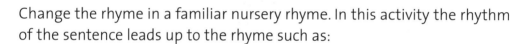

Change the rhyme in a familiar nursery rhyme. In this activity the rhythm of the sentence leads up to the rhyme such as:

'Humpty Dumpty sat on a log
Humpty Dumpty jumped like a ... frog'

The child can submit the ending when they feel confident enough to do so. For children who struggle with this activity, use picture prompts. In the above example you could hold up three pictures, of a cog, a frog, and a kangaroo. The child could then point to the most appropriate picture to make a rhyme.

Activity 38:

Rhyme ball

The adult throws the ball to the child and says a word such as *pin*. The child throws the ball back to the adult and says a word that rhymes, such as *thin*. This continues until the adult changes to a different rhyme.

You will need:
a ball, a list of rhyming words (*see Resource sheets 2.4 and 2.5*)

Activities for older children at school

To be able to carry out the following activity the child should be able to write and read all the letters, and preferably some consonant clusters (bl, fl, st).

Activity 39:
Alphabet arc rimes

Set out the alphabet arc as shown below (see also Section 3, p64).

abcdefghijklmnopqrstuvwxyz

In the centre of the arc, place a rime (for example -at, -it, -en, -ad, -ip). The child should go around the arc trying each letter in front of the rime to see if it makes a proper word.

Extension
Give the child a selection of consonant clusters (placed above the arc) to generate more words.

Give the child more complex rimes (for example -ack, -ill, -iff, and -ump).

Ask the child to record on paper the list of words made.

Eventually this exercise can be carried out on paper by giving the child a sheet with the alphabet arc and any clusters on it. Put the rime or rimes in the middle of the arc with space for the child to write the newly generated words underneath.

Photocopiable resource sheets for Section 2: **Rhyming**

☐ **2.1: Rhyming skills checklist**

☐ **2.2: Three nursery rhymes**

☐ **2.3: Three more nursery rhymes**

☐ **2.4: Rhyming words A**

☐ **2.5: Rhyming words B**

☐ **2.6: Rhyming word picture cards A**

☐ **2.7: Rhyming word picture cards B**

☐ **2.8: Rhyming word picture cards C**

☐ **2.9: Rhyming word picture cards D**

☐ **2.10: Rhyming word picture cards E**

☐ **2.11A: Rhyming chain game A**

☐ **2.11B: Rhyming chain game B**

☐ **2.12: Rhyming bingo baseboard A**

☐ **2.13: Rhyming bingo baseboard B**

☐ **2.14: Rhyme in print – suggested reading**

Resource Sheet 2.1: **Rhyming skills checklist**

Name _____ Class _____

SECTION 2

Date	Activity	Comments
5/6	Reciting nursery rhymes	Can accurately recite 'Humpty Dumpty' and 'Twinkle twinkle', but replaces 'crown' with 'crowd' in 'Jack and Jill'.

Resource Sheet 2.2: **Three nursery rhymes**
(Activity 18)

Jack and Jill

Jack and Jill went up the hill
To fetch a pail of water
Jack fell down and broke his crown
And Jill came tumbling after

Pat a cake

Pat a cake, pat a cake, baker's man
Bake me a cake as fast as you can
Pat it and prick it and mark it with B
And put it in the oven for Baby and me

Hey diddle diddle

Hey diddle diddle, the cat and the fiddle
The cow jumped over the moon
The little dog laughed to see such sport
And the dish ran away with the spoon

Resource Sheet 2.3: **Three more nursery rhymes**
(Activity 18)

The Queen of Hearts

The Queen of Hearts, she made some tarts
All on a summer's day
The Knave of Hearts, he stole the tarts
And took them clean away

Little Boy Blue

Little Boy Blue
Come blow on your horn
The sheep's in the meadow
The cow's in the corn
But where is the boy
Who looks after the sheep
He's under a haycock
Fast asleep

There was a crooked man

There was a crooked man
And he walked a crooked mile
He found a crooked sixpence against a crooked stile
He bought a crooked cat, which caught a crooked mouse
And they all lived together in a little crooked house

Resource Sheet 2.4: **Rhyming words A**
(Activities 23, 28, 38)

match	sing	cake
patch	ring	rake
catch	wing	lake
hatch	thing	snake
flag	lock	tree
bag	sock	see
rag	clock	knee
tag	block	free
stamp	duck	bear
lamp	truck	chair
camp	luck	hair
damp	muck	fair
well	moon	frog
bell	spoon	dog
sell	soon	log
tell	noon	bog
kick	cat	pool
tick	mat	cool
sick	bat	fool
trick	hat	school

Resource Sheet 2.5: **Rhyming words B**

(Activities 23, 28, 38)

van	chin	drink
man	pin	wink
pan	bin	sink
can		
	dig	frog
match	pig	dog
catch	wig	log
patch		
	kick	bug
head	tick	jug
bread	lick	rug
shed		
bed		
	ship	snake
	clip	rake
bell	zip	cake
shell		lake
well		
	sing	
	wing	clown
pen	sling	crown
hen	ring	town
ten		
men		
	lock	knee
	sock	tree
nest	clock	three
vest	block	key

Resource Sheet 2.6: **Rhyming word picture cards A**
(Activities 24, 28, 29)

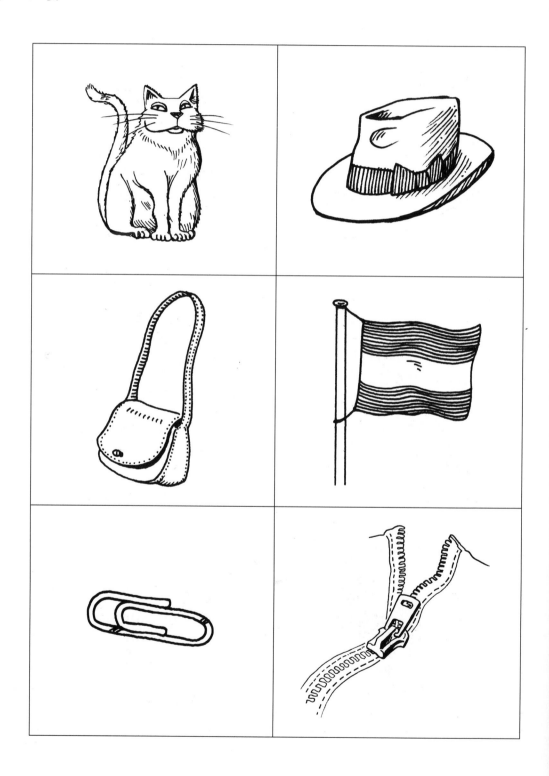

Resource Sheet 2.7: **Rhyming word picture cards B**
(Activities 24, 28, 29)

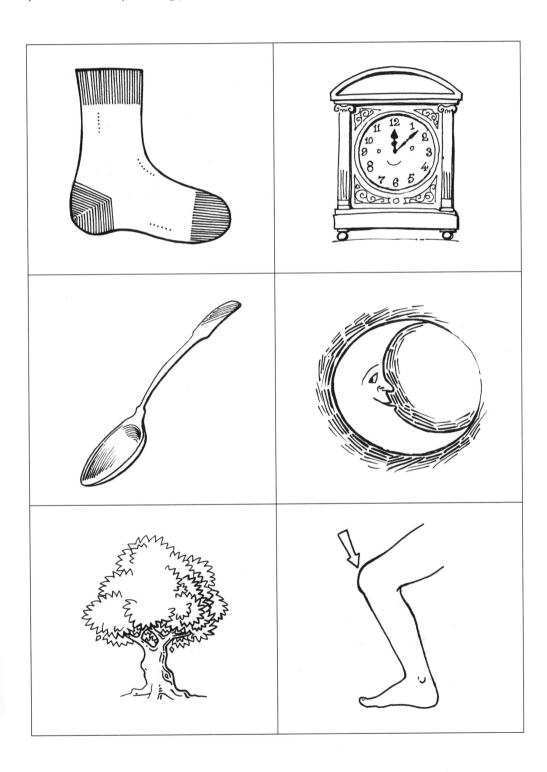

Resource Sheet 2.8: **Rhyming word picture cards C**
(Activities 24, 28, 29)

Resource Sheet 2.9: **Rhyming word picture cards D**
(Activities 24, 28, 29)

Resource Sheet 2.10: **Rhyming word picture cards E**
(Activities 24, 28, 29)

Resource Sheet 2.11A: **Rhyming chain game A**
(Activity 33)

Directions for use

- Cut out the paired pictures, fold them down the middle, and glue them back to back. (Or, if you prefer, you can stick the paired images on either side of a blank card.)
- Colour green the dots where shown in the top right-hand corner of the picture.

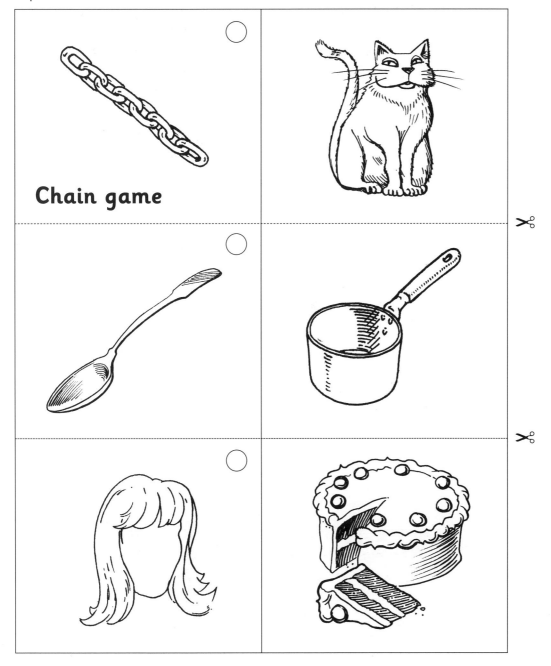

Chain game

SECTION 2

Resource Sheet 2.11B: **Rhyming chain game B**
(Activity 33)

Directions for use
- Cut out the paired pictures, fold them down the middle, and glue them back to back. (Or, if you prefer, you can stick the paired images on either side of a blank card.)
- Colour green the dots where shown in the top right-hand corner of the picture.

Resource Sheet 2.12: **Rhyming bingo baseboard A**
(Activity 24)

Directions for use

- Photocopy *Resource sheets 2.12* and *2.13* so that each child has one baseboard.
- Photocopy an extra copy of each, and cut it up to make separate cards.
- Follow the instructions for playing the game, as described on p30.

Resource Sheet 2.13: **Rhyming bingo baseboard B**
(Activity 24)

Directions for use: see *Resource sheet 2.12.*

Resource Sheet 2.14:
Rhyme in print – suggested reading

Books with a strong rhyme and rhythm

Ahlberg A, 1999, *The Jolly Postman*, Viking Children's Books, London.

Alborough J, 2004, *Where's my Teddy?*, Walker Books Ltd, London.

Alborough J, 2005, *Duck's Key*, HarperCollins Children's Books, London.

Beaton C, 2001, *How Big is a Pig?*, Barefoot Books, Bath.

Blackstone S, 2005, *My Granny went to Market*, Barefoot Books, Bath.

Donaldson J, 1999, *The Gruffalo*, Macmillan Children's Books, London.

Dr Seuss, 2003, *The Cat in the Hat*, HarperCollins Children's Books, London.

Dr Seuss, 2003, *Green Eggs and Ham*, Collins Picture Lions, London.

Dodd L, 2005, *Hairy Maclary*, Puffin Books, London.

Edwards R, 1997, *Nonsense Nursery Rhymes*, Oxford University Press, Oxford.

Hayes S, 2001, *This is the Bear*, Walker Books Ltd, London.

Hutchins P, 2002, *Don't Forget the Bacon*, Red Fox, London.

Collections of nursery rhymes and rhyming poems

Opie I, 1996, *My Very First Mother Goose*, Walker Books Ltd, London.

MacDonald Denton K, 2004, *A Child's Treasury of Nursery Rhymes* with audio CD, Kingfisher, London.

Jaques F, 1990 *The Orchard Book of Nursery Rhymes*, Orchard Books, London.

Sheridan S & Hibbert J, 1995, *Sing a Song of Sixpence: 60 Favourite Nursery Rhymes*, BBC Audio Books Young Collection, London.

Williams S, 1999, *Round and Round the Garden*, Oxford University Press, Oxford.

SECTION 3

Learning the alphabet

SECTION 3

Photocopiable resource sheets

Introduction

To communicate spoken language in written form a child must learn that the sounds in words (phonemes) are represented by letters or groups of letters (graphemes). Recognition of these letters enables a child to read and spell fluently. Learning the alphabet thoroughly is vital for a child to learn to read and spell. When beginning this process the child does not necessarily need to link the letters in the alphabet to the sounds they make. Instead the alphabet can be learned as a rote learning process.

Learning letters in sequence

The alphabet is necessary for many filing systems (dictionaries, reference books, phone books and so on), and therefore it is important that it is learnt in its correct order. This can be a daunting task for those with any kind of sequencing difficulty. Many children may pick up alphabetical order by singing an alphabet song without needing to make direct links to letter shapes. However, to ensure an accurate knowledge of the alphabet, concrete materials such as wooden letters should be used.

Frequently asked questions

Why should we use letter names rather than sounds for alphabet work?
In the initial stages of learning, alphabet sequencing is kept separate from phonological or sound awareness work – although, in time, children need to know the name, sound and sequence for each letter. Use *Resource sheet 3.13* either to record what has been taught or as an assessment to see which names and sounds are known. Using names for the letters at the beginning avoids confusion whilst work on letter sounds through oral phonics is happening simultaneously. (Please refer to the section on phonological awareness, pages 85 to 104, for further clarification.) When using the alphabet – for looking things up in dictionaries for example – we use names of letters.

How can I utilise the environment when working on the alphabet?

Many children pick up information about letters from their environment at a young age. Often common letters are recognised – for example, 'm' for 'McDonalds' – or they may have become aware of the first letter of their name. Young children tend to recognise upper case letters more easily as these are less confusing and are more recognisable in the environment.

Is it beneficial to learn the 'alphabet song'?

Many children know the 'alphabet song' but are confused around the 'l m n o p' section. It is important to be able to match the names of the letters to the symbols and to be secure with alphabetical order for purposes mentioned previously.

If children know an alphabet song, first get them to say the alphabet slowly to assess where any difficulties may lie. Singing the alphabet is a good way to help children learn it. However, use a variation on the traditional song that avoids the 'l m n o p' difficulties: the one on *Resource sheet 3.2* is ideal.

Teaching guidelines

1 Assess where the child is in terms of his knowledge of the alphabet by asking him to recite it first, then to lay it out using wooden letters.
2 Start slowly, teaching the first four letters, then adding to them. Do not try to teach the child the entire sequence at once.
3 If a child is finding it hard to remember the name for a letter, or is confusing two letters, place the letter in a feely bag or blindfold the child and get him to feel it whilst saying the name of the letter.

Remember

1 Be positive.
2 Model the activity for the child.
3 Use letter names when learning the alphabet.
4 Use the environment to find letters.
5 Use the Alphabet checklist (*Resource sheet 3.1*) to keep a record of the child's progress.

Playing with letters

Children need to learn to recognise the alphabet in both upper and lower case. The following activities will help children to link the letter shapes to the name of the letter and can be done with upper or lower case letters. The aim is for the child to know that the shapes 'A' and 'a' are both called 'a'. Linking the sounds to the letter shapes is addressed in the phonological awareness section (see pages 85 to 104).

Activities for school and home

Activity 40:
Printing letters

As the child prints letters, the adult says the name of the letter.

> **You will need:**
> letter shapes (sponge, foam, wooden, magnetic), a tray, paint

Variation
If the child confuses or is unsure of certain letters, then limit this activity to using only those particular letters.

Extension
If the child is fairly secure with the letter names, ask him to print specific letters called out at random.

Activity 41:
Growing letters

Mould the cotton wool strips to form letter shapes. Dampen them and sprinkle on cress seeds. Leave them for a few days in a light place. Watch the letters grow.

> **You will need:**
> cotton wool strips, water, cress seeds

SECTION 3

Activity 42:
Tactile letters

Make letters from a variety of materials including:

- kitchen foil – this can be rolled and scrunched
- pipe cleaners
- clay
- art straws.

Using pre-cut card letters stick on some of the following:

- wool
- velvet
- sand
- glitter
- sequins
- flattened kitchen foil
- fine sandpaper
- natural materials, such as leaves and small twigs.

Activity 43:
Initial letters

Children identify the initial letters of their names and make a collage of these letters using some of the above materials. These can be mounted on the wall in school or turned into a plaque for their bedroom door at home.

Activities for home

Activity 44:
Cooking letters

Bake biscuits using alphabet cookie cutters. Toast can also be cut with these.

There are some food brands that make letter shapes from foods – for example, potatoes and spaghetti.

You will need:
biscuit recipe,
ingredients and cutters

Activity 45:
Playdough letters

Playdough can be rolled to form letter shapes or alphabet cutters can be used to cut out letter shapes.

Activity 46:
Magnetic letters

These can be bought in small and large sizes and are useful to have on a fridge or freezer door.

Activity 47:
Bathtime letters

Foam letter shapes are available that can float in the bath, and you and your child can play games with these. For example, if you have a small fishing net, the child can try to catch the letter shapes that make up their name. Many of these letters also stick to the sides of the bath, so you can play bathtime games such as squirting certain letters with a water pistol, making real and nonsense words, etc.

SECTION 3

abcdefghijklmnopqrstuvwxyz

Alphabet arc

The alphabet arc is a multi-sensory technique for learning the sequence of the alphabet. The letters are set out in their correct order in a rainbow shape. This shape is ideal as the child can see, reach and easily manipulate the arc.

Activities 48–55 below use 3–D letters. Many of the activities described in the rest of this section make use of alphabet cards. Please note that *Resource sheets 3.11* and *3.12* provide sets of cards that will be ideal for many of these activities. Photocopy them onto card and then laminate them so that they may be reused as necessary.

An alphabet arc checklist has also been provided so that you can keep a note of each child's progress. For easy reference, this appears at the end of the Resources section, as *Resource sheet 3.13*.

Activities for school and home

Activity 48:
Alphabet arc

Work with upper-case letters to set out the alphabet rainbow – explain that there are twenty six letters in the alphabet, identify the beginning ('a') and end ('z') and, locate the middle ('m' and 'n').

Initially, the child may need to match letters onto a pre-drawn board. Use a large piece of card and draw around the letters in the arc. Allow the child to help you set out the arc of letters over a long period of time. Some children may take many weeks to do this: build up about four letters at a time and do not move on until the child has secure knowledge of them. Once the arc is set out, get the child to check

You will need:
a set of large 3-D upper- and lower-case letters in a non-cursive style (no flicks). These need to be large enough for children to feel the shape of the letters, but not so large that they are unmanageable – wooden ones are preferable, as they are more tactile

for any mistakes, such as reversals or putting the letters in the wrong order. By identifying his own mistakes he is less likely to repeat them next time. If he does not identify an error, quietly change the letters yourself without drawing too much attention to it – thereby keeping the experience as positive as possible.

Point to each letter in the arc as the child says the letter name. The child can sing the song if he wishes, but it is essential for his finger to keep up with the song! Once the child is secure with the upper-case alphabet, match the lower-case alphabet to it. After a while you can just use the lower-case letters.

Extension
As an extension activity you can time your child setting out the arc – aim for about one minute. Record the child's times on a 'personal best' chart, so whenever his speed improves the achievement can be recorded.

Activity 49:
Alphabet dominoes

When your child can put the arc out quickly and accurately, try playing alphabet dominoes as an alternative way of setting out the arc. This game should be played in pairs only.

> **You will need:**
> a set of large lower-case letters in a non-cursive style

The players take 13 letters each, and the player with 'm' starts. The next player can only put down a letter that is adjacent to 'm' – and so on.

Activity 50:
Imaginary alphabet

Give the child the letters of the alphabet at random, and ask him to put them in approximately the correct place in the arc. This builds the child's knowledge of the correct placement of each letter in the alphabet. This activity must only be undertaken if you are sure that the child is secure at putting out the arc correctly in order.

> **You will need:**
> a set of large lower-case letters in a non-cursive style

The games for activities 51 to 54 can be played once the alphabet arc has been set out.

Activity 51:
Letter swap

Blindfold the child and swap over two of the letters. Then remove the child's blindfold and ask him to guess which ones you have moved. Letters such as 'b' and 'd', 'g' and 'j', 'n' and 'u', 'u' and 'y', and 'i' and 'j' often cause confusion – either because they can *sound* similar in some words or because they are *visually* similar.

You will need:
a blindfold, a rainbow arc

Activity 52:
Pirates

Blindfold the child and remove a letter, then close up the gap. Remove the child's blindfold and ask him to put the pirate picture in the place that he thinks you stole the letter from!

You will need:
a small picture of a pirate (photocopied from *Resource sheet 3.3*), and a blindfold

Variation
Use a cut-out burglar, fairy or any other character that the child likes.

Activity 53:
Chunking

This technique will help children to develop the skills necessary for syllable segmentation, which is a useful spelling technique. Use the alphabet rainbow arc.

You will need:
a box with a hole in the side, small toys and objects, a list of rhyming words *(see Resource sheets 2.4 and 2.5)*

- Take turns to point to each letter in sequence and say its name.
- Next you say two letters and the child says the next two.
- Eventually the child should be able to work with chunks of three letters with stresses at different points – for example, 'a*bc*', 'd*ef*'.

Activity 54:
Pick-up game

To encourage short-term memory skills in the child, build this activity up very slowly – start with three letters and aim to achieve six – although this may take some time.

- Say the letter names with a one-second interval between each. Always give letters in alphabetical order
- The child should repeat the sequence of letters out loud
- The child should then pick out the letters in the correct sequence
- This is a good way to put away the letters.

Variation
You can vary this activity by making cards of the sequence of letters and showing them to the child for between three and six seconds each. This works on the child's visual memory rather than on his auditory memory.

Letter identification

Activities for school and home

Activity 55:
Feely bag

Identify between four and six letters and put them into a feely bag. The child must feel and then name each letter. He earns a counter for each letter that is identified correctly. If several children are playing, the first to earn six counters is the winner. If the child is really secure with the alphabet, you can play a game where you both pull a letter out of the bag and the one which is closest to 'a' (or 'z') is the winner.

You will need:
a set of large 3-D lower-case letters in a non-cursive style, a feely bag (a cloth bag with a drawstring opening), 12 counters

Activity 56:
Spotty monsters

Each child takes turns to pick a card. If the child can identify the letter correctly by name then they can cover a spot with a counter. The first child to complete his board is the winner. You can make a wide variety of these boards by drawing a shape or picture and marking the outline with 26 circles, stars, etc.

You will need:
1 set of alphabet cards, 26 counters, 1 spotty monster base board per player (take photocopies of *Resource sheet 3.4*)

Activity 57:
Alphabet snakes

This is a game for two players. First, choose the colour of counter for each player. Each player takes turns to pick an alphabet card. If the player can identify it correctly he can use one of his counters to cover the correct space on the board. If the letter is covered already, he misses a turn. When the snake is covered in counters the person with the most coloured counters on the snake is the winner.

You will need:
a snake baseboard with the sequence of the alphabet on it (photocopied from *Resource sheet 3.5*), two sets of alphabet cards shuffled, counters in two colours

Activity 58:
Alphabet pairs

Turn the cards face down. Take turns to try and find a pair of matching cards. To extend this use sets of upper-case and lower-case letters – put a different coloured spot on the back of the lower-case and upper-case cards to distinguish between them.

You will need:
two sets of alphabet cards

Activity 59:
Alphabet bingo

Photocopy *Resource sheet 3.6*, and laminate it, then cut it in two. Each photocopy makes boards for two players. With a dry-wipe marker, write on to the blank bingo board some of the letters of the alphabet. Ensure that you include a mixture of those that the child recognises easily and a few that they find hard. Using a feely bag, let the child pull letters out of the bag. If the child identifies them on their card and can say the name correctly, then put a counter on the card. The first child to get a line or complete their card is the winner.

You will need:
a laminated blank bingo card for each player (photocopied from *Resource sheet 3.6*), a dry-wipe marker, a feely bag, a set of large lower-case letters in a non-cursive style

Activity 60:
Letter name fishing game

Take turns to fish for the letters. If the child can identify the letter they catch, they can keep it; if not, it goes back in the pond. If this game is played one-to-one with an adult, the adult can keep the ones the child does not know. The one with the most fish at the end is the winner.

You will need:
paper fish (see *Resource sheet 3.7*) photocopied onto card and cut out. Add one letter (lower-case, upper-case or both) per fish, written or printed on. Paper clips to attach to each fish. A fishing rod (a stick or pencil with string and a small magnet on the end), a piece of blue cloth or a tray for the pond

SECTION 3

Activity 61:
Join the dots

These sheets require the child to join the dots in the sequence of the alphabet. Encourage the child to verbalise what he is doing – it is a fun way to recite the alphabet! There are puzzle books available that include alphabet dot-to-dot sheets, although some are very small for young children and would need enlarging.

You will need:
alphabet dot-to-dot sheets (photocopies of *Resource sheets 3.8, 3.9* and *3.10*), a pencil

Activities for home

Activity 62:
Letters all around

Identify letters in the environment: for example, on road signs, shop signs and packaging.

Activity 63:
Counting letters

- On car journeys, look at number plates and try to count how many number plates have the letter that begins the child's name
- Count how many examples of a certain letter there are on the way to school
- Look at a list of friends' names. Think of ways of sorting the names using their initial letters.

Activity 64:
Baking letters

Use alphabet cookie cutters to make biscuits. Allow the child to eat the biscuit if he can name the letter.

Variation
Use the cutters with rolled-out icing and make slogans to spell out on cakes, or initial letters for individual cakes.

You will need:
biscuit recipe, ingredients and alphabet cutters

Photocopiable resource sheets for Section 3:
Learning the alphabet

☐ **3.1: Alphabet checklist**

☐ **3.2: Alphabet song**

☐ **3.3: Pirate for use with the alphabet arc**

☐ **3.4: Spotty monster baseboard**

☐ **3.5: Alphabet snake baseboard**

☐ **3.6: Alphabet bingo – blank boards**

☐ **3.7: Letter name fishing game A**

☐ **3.8: Alphabet dot-to-dot A**

☐ **3.9: Alphabet dot-to-dot B**

☐ **3.10: Alphabet dot-to-dot C**

☐ **3.11: Lower-case letter cards**

☐ **3.12: Upper-case letter cards**

☐ **3.13: Alphabet arc checklists**

SECTION 3

Resource Sheet 3.1: **Alphabet checklist**

Name _____   Class _____

Date	Activity	Comments
6/9	Laying out alphabet arc	See alphabet arc checklist (Resource sheet 3.14). Set out arc to 'p'. Reversed 'f' and 'j' and confused 'l,m,n,o' section. Use feely bag next time to distinguish 'l,m,n,o'.

Resource Sheet 3.2: **Alphabet song**

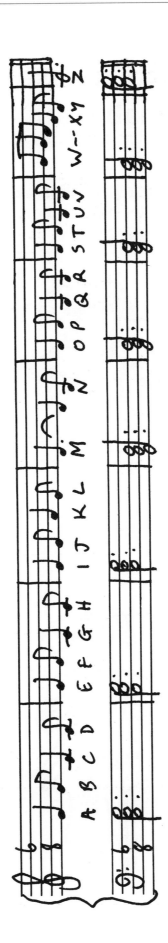

SECTION 3

Resource Sheet 3.3: **Pirate for use with the**
(Activity 52) **alphabet arc**

Directions for use

- Photocopy this page on to card and cut it to make six pirates
- Invite the children to colour the pirates in differently, if desired

Resource Sheet 3.4: **Spotty monster baseboard**
(Activity 56)

Resource Sheet 3.5: **Alphabet snake baseboard**
(Activity 57)

Resource Sheet 3.6: **Alphabet bingo – blank boards**
(Activity 59)

Resource Sheet 3.7: **Letter name fishing game**
(Activity 60)

Directions for use

- Take two photocopies of this sheet. Either copy each sheet onto card, or glue it onto card after copying. You will then have enough fish to use one for each letter of the alphabet.
- Write the desired letters or words onto the fish. After you have done this, you may wish to consider laminating the cards to make them more durable.
- Cut out the fish and attach a paper clip to each one.
- Find a small stick or pencil which you can use to make the fishing rod. Attach a piece of string to one end of the rod. Tie a small magnet to the loose end of the string.
- Create a pond using a piece of blue cloth or card, placed on the surface of a tray. Play the game as directed on page 69.

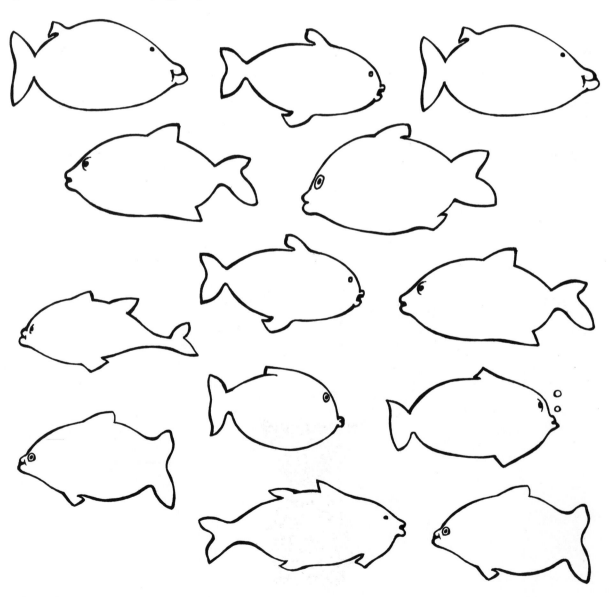

Resource Sheet 3.8: **Alphabet dot-to-dot A**
(Activity 61)

What to do
Join up the letters, starting with the letter 'a' and working through the whole alphabet.

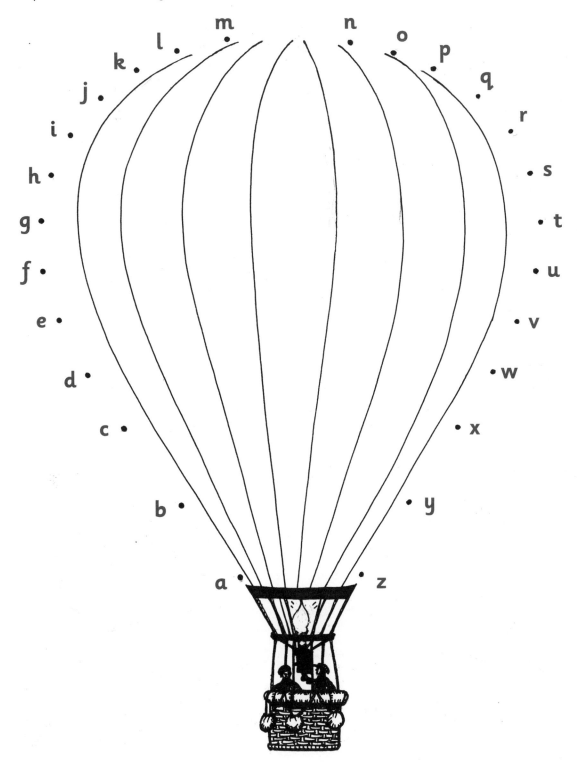

SECTION 3

Resource Sheet 3.9: **Alphabet dot-to-dot B**

(Activity 61)

What to do

Make this umbrella bigger by joining up the letters. Start with the letter 'a' and work through the whole alphabet.

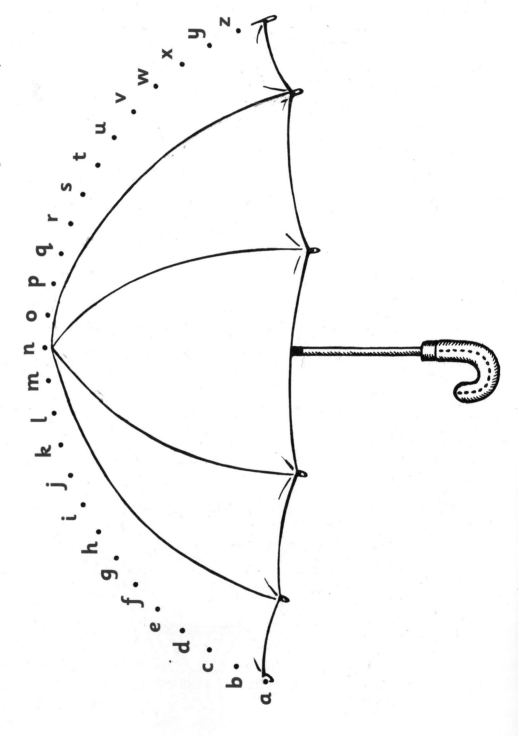

Resource Sheet 3.10: **Alphabet dot-to-dot C**
(Activity 61)

What to do
Join up the letters, starting with the letter 'a' and working through the whole alphabet.
You will make a picture of something. Can you guess what?

SECTION 3

Resource Sheet 3.11: **Lower-case letter cards**
(Activities 56, 57, 58)

a	b	c	d
e	f	g	h
i	j	k	l
m	n	o	p
q	r	s	t
u	v	w	x
y	z		

Resource Sheet 3.12: **Upper-case letter cards**
(Activities 56, 57, 58)

A	B	C	D
E	F	G	H
I	J	K	L
M	N	O	P
Q	R	S	T
U	V	W	X
Y	Z		

SECTION 3

Resource Sheet 3.13: **Alphabet arc checklist**

Directions for use

Use this sheet when checking knowledge of letter names and sounds by pointing to a letter and asking for its sound, or asking children to pick a wooden letter and give its name.

Date checked: _____

Letter name	a	b	c	d	e	f	g	h	i	j	k	l	m	n	o	p	q	r	s	t	u	v	w	x	y	z	
Sound																											

Date checked: _____

Letter name	a	b	c	d	e	f	g	h	i	j	k	l	m	n	o	p	q	r	s	t	u	v	w	x	y	z	
Sound																											

Date checked: _____

Letter name	a	b	c	d	e	f	g	h	i	j	k	l	m	n	o	p	q	r	s	t	u	v	w	x	y	z	
Sound																											

SECTION 4

Phonological
awareness

SECTION 4

Introduction

Phonological awareness is the ability to identify sounds and, in particular, the sounds within words. Phonology deals with speech sounds. Phonics is a common term for linking sounds with letters and letter strings and is a way of teaching reading and spelling. Without a good phonological awareness many children struggle with phonics. It is therefore crucial for young children to understand that speech is made up of words and that those words can be broken down into *phonemes* (units of sound). They must then learn the *graphemes* (letters and letter strings) that represent these units of sound if they are to be able to read or spell fluently.

The alphabet is a series of twenty-six letters that consists of five vowels and twenty-one consonants. The vowels are important as, when saying them aloud, children may be encouraged to use both the vowel *name* (a long vowel) and its *sound* (a short vowel). When breaking words down into syllables, each syllable must contain a vowel. (The letter 'y' is a 'part-time' vowel and is usually used as a substitute for 'i' or 'e'.)

Work on rhyme will give children a basic understanding of sounds within words and phonics work will benefit from this. However, the best way to teach phonics is frequently the subject of debate.

Synthetic phonics

Synthetic phonics is a system where children learn up to 44 phonemes and their related graphemes (the written representations of the sound). They are then taught to sound out each phoneme in the word, blending them together to pronounce the word phonetically. This approach works very well if the word is phonetically regular. It is often implemented by introducing five or six sounds over a short space of time and repeating them frequently. Once they are secure, more may be introduced. This is done using a multi-sensory technique of seeing the symbol, listening to the sound, saying the sound and doing an action to represent the sound.

Analytic phonics

Analytic phonics is a system where whole words are analysed to find phonetic patterns. They are then broken down into smaller parts to help decode the word. Using onset and rime (see rhyming skills section and frequently asked questions below) is an example of this. Using the onset and rime approach can be beneficial for children to ensure that they gain a wide 'sight' vocabulary: for example, if they learn 'could' they can then tackle 'should' and 'would' with ease.

A combined approach

In practice, learners need to engage with both approaches to become successful readers and spellers. There is no single system that will enable all the words of our language to be read or spelt correctly. Different learners will require more emphasis on different techniques. Including both approaches in a multi-sensory approach is the most efficient way to encourage the development of reading and writing in young children.

Frequently asked questions

Why teach syllable segmentation first?
Syllables are the easiest segments in speech to distinguish. We sometimes use the term 'beating out' when referring to syllable division. It is much easier to break a word such as 'dreaming' into two syllables (dream / ing) than to work out the individual phonemes – units of sound – within it (d – r – ea – m – i – ng).

Segmenting words syllable by syllable ensures that children attend to their sound structure.

What are onset and rime?
The onset is the first part of the word and the rime is the end sound, for example:

   c (onset) + at (rime) = cat

'Awareness of onset–rime division before the child formally encounters letters and letter patterns provides a firm foundation for, not merely a bridge to later reading and spelling' (Layton et al, 1999).

SECTION 4

My child does not seem to be progressing with phonics: what shall I do?
First, it is important to rule out a hearing loss. This is very common in young children and you need to refer to the child's general practitioner (GP) or health visitor if you are concerned.

Some children appear to be coping with phonological awareness and rhyming activities but when you listen carefully to their individual responses in language games, this may not be the case. Make sure that you check individuals so that children who murmur along with a group do not slip through the net.

What are 'pure' sounds and why should we use them in all phonics teaching?
Pure sounds are, as they seem – the purest form of the sound. Sounds are written in / / marks to denote them from the written grapheme. Consonants should always be pure sounds. However many adults, and therefore the children they teach, add an /uh/ sound or 'schwah' to the end of each sound. It is crucial to take each sound back to its purest form: for example, /sss/ not /suh/ for the symbol 's'. Similarly, the pure sound for 'x' is /ks/, as heard at the end of the words box and fox.

If you are trying to discover the pure sound there are two main methods.

1 Say the word slowly (as though you were a robot). For example:
    /kw/ /ē/ /n/ for queen
    /ch/ /a/ /m/ /p/ for champ.

2 Listen to the sound as it occurs at the end of the word. For example: sit should be /s/ /i/ /t/ not /s/ /i/ /tuh/.

If pure sounds are taught it will make spelling a simpler process as you are not adding the confusing schwah, which can lead to incorrect spellings (such as cuatu for cat).

What are long and short vowel sounds?
Vowels are the only letters that can 'say' their name as well as their sound. The long vowel sounds are denoted by a symbol called a macron. A macron is a straight line above the character.

- /ā/ for acorn
- /ē/ for equals
- /ī/ for iron
- /ō/ for open
- /ū/ for uniform.

The short vowel sounds are denoted by a symbol called a breve. A breve is a cup shape placed above the letter.

- /ă/ for apple
- /ŏ/ for orange
- /ĕ/ for egg
- /ŭ/ for umbrella
- /ĭ/ for ink

Young children do not need to know these symbols but it can be useful for them to understand them if they have difficulties at a later stage.

What are digraphs?
Digraphs are where two letters represent one sound. For example: in *thin* the /th/ sound is represented by 't' and 'h'; in *rain* the /ā/ sound is represented by 'a' and 'i'; in *much* the /ch/ sound is represented by 'c' and 'h'.

Teaching guidelines

1 Carry out activities in a quiet area if at all possible.
2 Check that the child does not have a hearing problem that requires medical attention.
3 Be aware of overlaps with reading and writing skills but try not to combine the skills before the child is ready.
4 Overlearning will be necessary at all stages.

Remember

1 Speak clearly.
2 Use pure sounds.
3 Use a multi-sensory approach.
4 Be positive.
5 Use the Phonological awareness checklist (*Resource sheet 4.1*) to keep a record of the child's progress.

SECTION 4

Identifying syllables

Model how to divide a word into syllables by clapping or beating a drum. Syllables can also be worked out by placing a hand under the chin and counting how many times the chin goes down: however, this is quite difficult for very young children.

Activities for school

Activity 65:
Greetings

When registering pupils or at the start of a work session greet the pupil and beat out the syllables in their name as you do so – then wait for a response. For example:

Teacher: 'Hello Thom/as, are you here today?'
Pupil: 'Hello everyone, Thom/as is here today.'

Activity 66:
Sentences

Take turns to choose different words to end a sentence such as, 'For break/fast we had saus/a/ges' or 'For break/fast we had ce/re/al'.

Activity 67:
Telling news using syllable division

'Yes/ter/day I went to Grand/ma's house for din/ner.'

Activity 68:
Making rhymes with words of two syllables or more

piglet/twiglet, flower/tower, water/daughter

Activities for school and home

Activity 69:
Beating out the syllables

Look at the objects or pictures and clap or beat out how many syllables are in the word. For example:

- boat (one syllable = one clap)
- wig/wam (two syllables)
- um/brel/la (three syllables)

This can be done in many ways – for example:

- Look at the picture and beat out the syllables.
- Look at the picture and point to a number card denoting the number of syllables.
- Adult points to a number and the child places on it a picture card with that number of syllables in the word.
- The child places the pictures in boxes individually marked 1, 2 or 3, according to the number of syllables in the name of the object shown.

> **You will need:**
> a collection of objects or pictures that represent objects of between one and three syllables as listed on *Resource sheet 4.2*, or you may prefer to use the ready-made syllable picture cards on *Resource sheets 4.3A* and *4.3B*; three boxes; three number cards numbered 1, 2 and 3

Activity 70:
Hearing syllables in speech

Robotic speech
Pretend to be a robot and speak with a robotic voice. This is effectively segmenting words into syllables.

Singing
Clap or beat a drum in time to music. Many songs involve different notes for each syllable: for example, 'Sing a song of sixpence'.

SECTION 4

Sound identification

Activities for school and home

Activity 71:
Tapping out the number of sounds

This activity is different from syllabification because here we are identifying individual units of sound. We can identify the units by tapping the sounds in a single word with two fingers in the palm of the hand, or by pushing on fingers to represent each sound. These actions distinguish the activity from the beating out used for syllable segmentation. All the same, it is wise to carry out these activities at a different time from the syllable activities to eliminate all possible confusion.

Begin with three sounds in consonant vowel consonant (cvc), words such as: c-a-t; p-i-g; m-e-n. Then build up to four sounds, and include digraphs – for example: frog; d-r-u-m; ch-a-m-p.

In words like 'flag' many children hear the beginning two letters as one sound. It is in fact two distinguishable sounds - unlike /ch/, which is two letters making one sound and is known as a digraph.

Activity 72:
Initial sound identification

- Give the child a picture card and ask him to identify the first sound he hears when he says the object on the picture card. For example, if the picture shows a pan the first sound is /p/.
- Say a word and ask the child to identify the first sound he hears in it.
- Point to a card – can the child find another that begins with the same sound?
- Make a collection of the picture cards showing objects whose names begin with the same sound.

Activity 73:
Final sound identification

- Give the child a picture card and ask him to identify the final sound he hears when he says the name of the object on the picture card. For example if the picture shows a pan, the last sound is /n/.
- Say a word and ask the child to identify the last sound he hears in it.
- Point to a card – ask the child to find another showing an object whose name ends with the same sound.
- Make a collection of the cards that end with the same sound.

Activity 74:
Medial sound identification

- Give the child a picture card and ask him to identify the middle (medial) sound he hears when he says the name of the object on the picture card – pan /ă/.
- Say a word and ask the child to identify the middle sound they hear in it.

Extension
If a child is able to, ask him to write the middle (medial) sounds on paper or on a whiteboard.

- Point to a card – can the child find another that has the same sound in the middle?
- Make a collection of the cards that have the same medial sound.

Activity 75:
The alliteration name game

Alliteration is a series of words beginning with the same sound. If you are working with a child on an individual basis, invite him to invent alliterative words to go with the names of people he knows.

A pleasant alliterative adjective is thought up for each child's name, for example:

- 'My name is jolly Jack.'
- 'My name is bouncy Bethany.'

SECTION 4

Activity 76:
The things I like game

This game further extends Activity 75. Think of things that each child or person likes, beginning with the initial letter of his name.

- 'Tom likes toes, treats, teddy and television.'
- 'Holly likes holidays, Harry and hopscotch.'

Activity 77:
Blending games

You say a series of sounds that make up a word (real or nonsense) and the child has to blend them together to form a word. For example:

- /b/ /ă/ /t/ – bat
- /b/ /ō/ /t/ – boat
- /f/ /r/ /ĭ/ /m/ – frim

Activities for older children at school

Activity 78:
Where does the sound come from?

To make progress with this activity a child must have a good understanding of the terms beginning, middle and end.

When you show a card you also say one of the sounds within the word. The child uses the beginning, middle and end board and points to the place where he heard the sound. This can be extended by using more complex words such as those containing the sound /sh/ as in push, shell, station.

> **You will need:**
> a beginning, middle and end board for each child (you can photocopy this from *Resource sheet 4.4* and colour the traffic lights appropriately); cvc (consonant – vowel – consonant) word picture cards, photocopied from *Resource sheet 4.5*

Activity 79:
Grids

Ask the child to write words by putting each sound in a separate square: use cvc and ccvc words only for this exercise. Here are some examples:

You will need:
large squared paper, pens

- c a t will take up three squares
- f r o g will take up four squares
- sh i p will take up three squares.

Extension
As children learn more graphemes that represent phonemes (for example, ll, ck, ff, ss, oa, and ai) this exercise can be extended to include more complex words.

Activity 80:
Change the sounds

Ask the child to write words but to change one of the phonemes. For example, you might tell the child:

You will need:
a whiteboard marker and pen

- 'Change pan to pat'
- 'Change luck to pluck'
- 'Write fort without the /t/'.

After each instruction, the child holds up the whiteboard to show you.

SECTION 4

Photocopiable resource sheets for Section 4:
Phonological awareness

☐ **4.1: Phonological awareness checklist**

☐ **4.2: One-, two- and three-syllable words**

☐ **4.3A: Syllable picture cards**

☐ **4.3B: Syllable picture cards**

☐ **4.4: Beginning, middle and end boards**

☐ **4.5: Consonant-vowel-consonant (CVC) word picture cards**

Resource Sheet 4.1: **Phonological awareness checklist**

Name _____ Class _____

Date	Activity	Comments
19/3	medial sound identification – collecting cards with the same medial sound (Activity 74)	Can sort /ă/ /ŏ/ and /ŭ/ medially but is confusing /ĕ/ and /ĭ/

SECTION 4

Resource Sheet 4.2: **One-, two- and three-syllable**
(Activity 69) **words**

One-syllable words	Two-syllable words	Three-syllable words
duck	flower	microwave
frog	ladder	crocodile
ring	whistle	elephant
cow	trailer	telephone
pen	tractor	dinosaur
book	glasses	wheelbarrow
bun	tissue	umbrella
cat	jumper	violin
twig	spider	ladybird
hat	sandwich	butterfly
snake	kettle	aeroplane
cup	window	umbrella
pig	baby	
bee	lighthouse	
boat	pencil	
	candle	
	wigwam	

Resource Sheet 4.3A: **Syllable picture cards A**
(Activity 69)

Resource Sheet 4.3B: **Syllable picture cards B**
(Activity 69)

Resource Sheet 4.4: **Beginning, middle and end boards**
(Activity 78)

Directions for use

- Photocopy this sheet on to card.
- Cut the sheet into two to make two separate boards.
- On each sheet, colour the traffic lights (from top to bottom) red, amber and green – or you might ask the child to do so.
- Play 'Where does the sound come from' – Activity 78, page 96.

Beginning	Middle	End

Beginning	Middle	End

SECTION 4

Resource Sheet 4.5: **consonant-vowel-consonant**
(Activity 78) **(CVC) word picture cards**

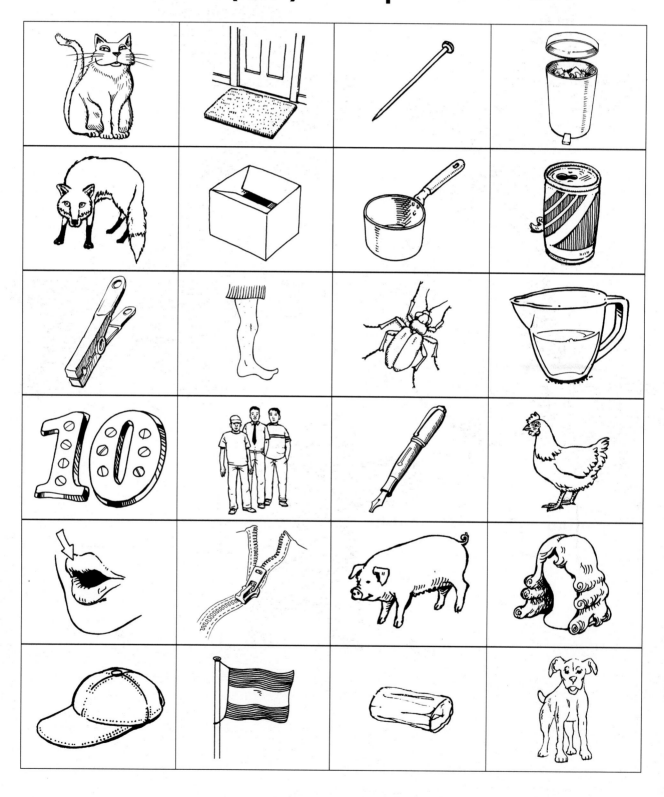

SECTION 5
Reading

SECTION 5

Introduction

Reading is a necessary life skill. We need it for essential purposes, such as reading labels on food and medicines, or following road signs. Many people feel that reading for pleasure is a wonderful experience that can further their knowledge and can transport them to places and worlds that they may never encounter normally. To succeed in school and in working life it is necessary to become a proficient reader.

Methods for the teaching of reading

Over the years many techniques for teaching reading have gone in and out of fashion but four key methods have remained.

1 The whole word method (sometimes called 'look and say') where the child is given words on flashcards and is expected to memorise them as a visual unit. Lists of common ('high-frequency') words, taken from the National Literacy Strategy framework for teaching (DfES, 1998) are provided on *Resource sheet 5.8*.
2 The 'phonics' method, where the child learns the sounds of the letters and decodes words by finding units of sounds.
3 The 'whole sentence' method, where the child is expected to read a sentence and use the meaning of the sentence to work out unfamiliar words. Cloze procedure is one example of this method: words are omitted from text and the reader is expected to insert a suitable word.
4 The 'alphabetic' method, where multi-sensory teaching of letters and sounds is combined and the child is expected to make a connection between the phonemes and graphemes to then read the words.

A combined approach

A strong emphasis on phonics is a priority for teaching children to read but it is important to understand the other approaches. Using a combination of these approaches, depending on the needs and strengths of the child, would seem the optimum way of helping children to become fluent readers. The section on phonological awareness (pages 85 to 104) introduced the idea that words are made up of individual sounds. To read fluently the child must then learn to match the sounds to written symbols (graphemes). This can be achieved through the use of approaches such as the Reading Pack (outlined in this section), published structured schemes such as *Jolly Phonics* (Lloyd, 1992) or through DfES publications such as *Playing with Sounds* (DfES, 2004).

Formal teaching of reading for many children starts in school. However, there are many key skills that can be encouraged at an earlier age that will ensure that the process of learning to read is much easier. If the child is keen to know what letters and words say, then follow his lead and begin helping him to develop his literacy skills.

Frequently asked questions

Should I worry if a child has no awareness of letters and words?
No. Many children under the age of five years do not notice the letters and words but are fascinated by the pictures and the storytelling, and your main aim should be to encourage this early love of books. If learning to decode words becomes a chore for the child, then you run the risk of putting him off reading. However, if you run your finger under the words as you read them, the child may come to realise that the symbols on the page and the words that you are saying are related.

What are formal 'reading books'?
'Reading scheme books' or 'graded word reading books' are books that have been specifically written to help with the teaching of reading. There are many published schemes available, and good nurseries and schools use a mixture of schemes, sometimes banded according to the level of difficulty. In the early stages, books with pictures and no words are useful for encouraging children to look carefully at detail and to think about what may happen next. At the next stage are books that are either based on repetition of sight words (common or 'high-frequency' words) or use a combination of cvc words (consonant-vowel-consonant words such as hot, dog, can) and simple sight words. These then introduce further letter combinations in line with the teaching of phonics. Each different scheme will have an approach that is either based on sight words or on phonics; most children need a combination of both.

When should a child start reading 'reading books'?

Books without any words can be shared at any age. To begin reading a phonics-based scheme, however, a child should know all his initial sounds. To begin reading a sight words scheme, he should know his sounds and also have been introduced to the particular sight words used in the book. However, some children are instinctive readers and will have demonstrated their natural reading ability by already reading words in their environment; these children too are ready to start reading books.

Should I cover the pictures when hearing a child read a graded word reading book?

No. Pictures are a useful tool to help the child decode the words and to understand the meaning in the stories. Encourage the child to look at the pictures before tackling the text.

Teaching guidelines

1 Be aware of the methods for teaching reading, particularly the teaching of phonics, and combine these with a book-rich environment.
2 Use the environment to show each child how useful reading can be.
3 Encourage a respect and love of books by making reading time special (whether you are reading stories or information books), modelling excitement and interest and taking care of books.

Remember

1 Wait until the child is ready before expecting him to read independently.
2 Model the uses for reading.
3 Be positive!
4 Use the Reading checklist (*Resource sheet 5.1*) to keep a record of the child's progress.

Sharing books together

Activities for School

Activity 81:
Using reading areas

Reading areas can be created in an area of the classroom to encourage children to sit and read quietly, alone or in pairs.

- Place cushions on the floor to make the area comfortable.
- Close the area off, either by using furniture or by creating a 'tent' with fabric or ribbons hung from the ceiling.
- Display books on a theme – for example, information books, pirate stories, or books by a favourite author or illustrator.
- Make displays on the walls of the book area to encourage children to use it. For example, you might display pictures of characters, posters advertising books, or photographs of children sharing a favourite book.
- Provide puppets or props to help tell familiar stories. For example, you might supply for the 'Three little pigs' story a puppet for each character and a bundle of sticks, straw and some small building bricks.

Activity 82:
Time to hear stories

- Make time, daily if possible, to sit quietly and read books individually or in pairs.
- Pair older children in the school with younger children and encourage them to share books together.
- Read aloud to children a book that they may not necessarily choose to read themselves.
- Encourage children to talk about the stories and characters, to predict endings and find similar poems or stories.

General activities for home

It is important that the child can maintain his attention for a whole story when sharing a short book with an adult, so choose a comfortable place with few distractions. Children learn best by copying the behaviour of others, so watching adults read a variety of material is very important. This may include reading novels or magazines for pleasure, newspapers for information, recipes or instructions to find out how to do something new. When sharing a book, create opportunities for discussion without distracting the child from the story. Children of five and under will probably prefer picture books. Books with flaps, pop-ups and tactile sections will be interesting to look at and may initially hold a child's attention a little longer than a simple picture book. Use the pictures to help with the story, either by silently pointing to things as you read or by prompting the child to look for clues to what may happen next or how a character may be feeling.

Book cover detectives

General activities for school and home *

Looking at books

Finding out together about the mechanics of the book will help the child when he chooses books in the future. Before opening the book, discuss some of the information on the cover. Ask, 'Where is the front of the book?' Then ask, 'How can we tell which way up the book goes?'

Always read the title and tell the child who the author is; for example, 'The author is … She is the person who wrote the book'. Also talk about the illustrator if appropriate. 'The man who illustrated the book, who drew the pictures, is …' Young children will soon understand these words and use them appropriately.

Choosing a book

When choosing a book you can refer to the blurb on the back, training children how to select books in the future. Ask the child to find other books by the same author, from a small selection. How does the child know that they are written (or illustrated) by the same person? Offer three books and ask the child to select one, giving a reason for his selection.

Talking about the content of the book

Predicting what might happen next is a crucial skill for any reader and picture books often give a lot of scope for practising this skill. Answering questions about a story or part of a story encourages the child to listen carefully. You can ask the child to ask you a question about the story, too: this is another way of ensuring that he has been paying attention. Use the question words 'who', 'when', 'why' and 'where' to find out whether the child has correctly understood character, time, plot and setting.

The child should be able to join in with repetition in a story if given the chance to do so. He should also be encouraged to provide or finish the rhyming word in a sentence or poem if you feel that he is able to do so.

SECTION 5

Sequencing

When you have finished reading the book, find out whether the child can recount one significant event, describe the main character, or continue the story further. For example, you might ask 'What happened after Goldilocks was chased away by the three bears? Where did she go? Who did she meet? Did she visit their house again?'

Eventually the child should be able to recount storylines in correct chronological sequence. You can further encourage correct sequencing by pegging pictures from the story in a sequence on a washing line to make a 'washing line story', or by drawing a road on a piece of paper and adding events from the story to make a 'story map'.

From story to play

Transferring characters from stories into play situations encourages children's imagination. Remember storytelling and listening to stories based either on recognisable texts or direct from imagination encourages good speaking and listening skills.

Book making

Activities for school and home

Activity 83:
Making story books

Make little books, either by stapling a few pages together or by cutting out and then stapling the pages so that the book is shaped like an object featured in the story (for example, a car, a teddy bear).

You will need:
paper, scissors, a stapler, pens and pencils

Give the child coloured crayons, pencils etc, and allow his imaginations free rein. You can scribe the story for them if they would like you to. Do not forget to put the author's and illustrator's names on the front!

Activity 84:
Making information books

- Sequence photographs from a trip or event such as a birthday party and add simple captions to read with the child.
- Collect information and pictures about a subject that interests the child: for example, cars, frogs or dinosaurs.
- When you have made your own books with the child, acknowledge them as real books by storing them on the bookshelf and sharing them together as you would any other book.

Activities for home

Activity 85:
Making alphabet books

Label each page of a scrapbook with the upper-case and lower-case version of each letter. Cut out and stick pictures onto each page to build a visual dictionary. Label the pictures in lower-case letters, if desired.

You will need:
a scrapbook, magazines and catalogues to make a collection of pictures of objects, scissors, glue, pens

SECTION 5

Identifying words

Children are aware that print is all around them in the environment. Many children will recognise familiar words, such as the names of shops or restaurants or road signs, particularly if someone has pointed them out. Gaining a sight vocabulary in this way is possible from a young age.

Activities for school and home

Activity 86:
Word walks

When going for a walk, look for familiar words; for example, road, street, bus stop.

Activity 87:
Everyday objects

Together, label familiar objects with both a word and a picture. If the child helps you to stick them on the appropriate item, he is more likely to refer to the label in future. For example: chair, table, desk, door.

You will need:
pieces of card, pens, Blu-Tack® (or something you can use to fix paper onto surfaces without damaging paint, etc)

Activity 88:
Tidying up

Label toy boxes and equipment areas with a word and a picture. If the box or piece of equipment is always kept in the same place (for example, on a shelf), label the shelf with an identical word and picture so that the child can match the two together.

Activity 89:
Play areas

Use written words within play situations. For example, if the play area is a make-believe restaurant, display 'Open' and 'Closed' signs, labels for the till, the toilets and the kitchen. Make menu cards for food, and put up a sign giving the name of the restaurant.

Activities for older children at school

Activity 90:
Sight words

Make cards with simple common words printed on them. These should be words that you expect the child to read as a visual unit. For example: 'the', 'said', 'Mummy', and the child's name. A list of words recommended by the National Literacy Strategy for Reception (ages 4–5), Year 1 (ages 5–6) and Year 2 (ages 6–7) is listed at the end of this section (see *Resource sheet 5.8*). Try the following activities using the word cards you have made:

- Introduce three words by reading each one aloud and showing the child the relevant word card at the same time. The child should look at the card and repeat the word. Repeat three times per card.
- Check the cards daily. If the child remembers the word, put a tick on the card. Once the card has three ticks, then a new card can be introduced, but you should continue to revise the old cards too.

Reading Pack

Activities for school and home

What is a Reading Pack?

A Reading Pack consists of twenty six cards, one for each letter of the alphabet. A matching lower- and upper-case letter is shown on the front of each card. On the back of the card showing the letters 'A' and 'a' will appear one 'clue' word each for words beginning with the sounds /ă/ and /ā/ – apple and apron – together with pictures of these objects. The remaining alphabet cards will work in a similar way.

The Reading Pack should include pure sounds only (as discussed in the phonological awareness section, pages 85 to 104): remember this if you decide to make your own set.

How does a Reading Pack work?

The Reading Pack introduces the idea that each sound in our language can be represented by a letter (*grapheme*) or sequence of letters. Daily practice with these cards should encourage sound–letter correspondence.

The pack will be most beneficial if the child has himself chosen the clue words. However, a set of pre-drawn cards is provided at the end of this section as an example (see *Resource sheets 5.2 to 5.7*).

Making a Reading Pack

You can put together your own Reading Pack by photocopying *Resource sheets 5.2 to 5.7*. The easiest way of producing the pack is to photocopy the two sheets marked 'A', so that they are on either side of a single sheet of card, and cut out the cards. Do the same with the sheets marked 'B' and 'C'. Alternatively, you can photocopy all the sheets separately. Then glue the two sheets marked 'A', so that they are back-to-back and cut out the cards; you can reinforce the cards using blank playing cards if you wish. Do the same with the sheets marked 'B' and 'C'.

If you are using the pack with a whole class or group, you may wish to use larger cards – A5 size, for example.

When to use the pack

If the child is secure with many of the previous activities in this book, the Reading Pack will be beneficial. However, this is a complex activity, and you must be led by the progress the child has made so far.

Activity 91:

Reading Pack routine

Show the child a card with the letter on it. Then ask the child to say the word indicated by the picture clue – let the child look at the word if he is not sure.

Then ask the child to say the initial letter sound – you can look together at the picture to check that the child is right.

You will need:

the Reading Pack as described above (see also *Resource sheets 5.2 to 5.7*); if you are making further cards of your own, you will need card, a black marker pen and some coloured pens

Extension

The pack is initially made using the letters 'a' to 'z'. It can be extended by adding further letter combinations, such as *sh*, *ch* and *th* and by moving on to long vowel sounds.

Photocopiable resource sheets for Section 5: **Reading**

☐   **5.1: Reading checklist**

☐   **5.2: Front of Reading Pack cards A**

☐   **5.3: Front of Reading Pack cards B**

☐   **5.4: Front of Reading Pack cards C**

☐   **5.5: Back of Reading Pack cards A**

☐   **5.6: Back of Reading Pack cards B**

☐   **5.7: Back of Reading Pack cards C**

☐   **5.8: High-frequency words for children aged 4–5 (Reception), 5–6 years (Year 1) and 6–7 years (Year 2)**

Resource Sheet 5.1: **Reading checklist**

Name _____   Class _____

Date	Activity	Comments
6/8	Book cover detectives (see page 113) – author and illustrator	Told me that an author writes the words and knows that an illustrator draws the pictures but cannot recall the word 'illustrator'.

Resource Sheet 5.2: **Front of Reading Pack cards A**
(Activity 91)

a A	b B	c C
d D	e E	f F
g G	h H	i I

Resource Sheet 5.3: **Front of Reading Pack cards B**
(Activity 91)

j _J	k _K	l _L
m _M	n _N	o _O
p _P	q _Q	r _R

Resource Sheet 5.4: **Front of Reading Pack cards C**
(Activity 91)

s S	t T	u U
V V	W W	X X
y Y	z Z	

Resource Sheet 5.5: **Back of Reading Pack cards A**
(Activity 91)

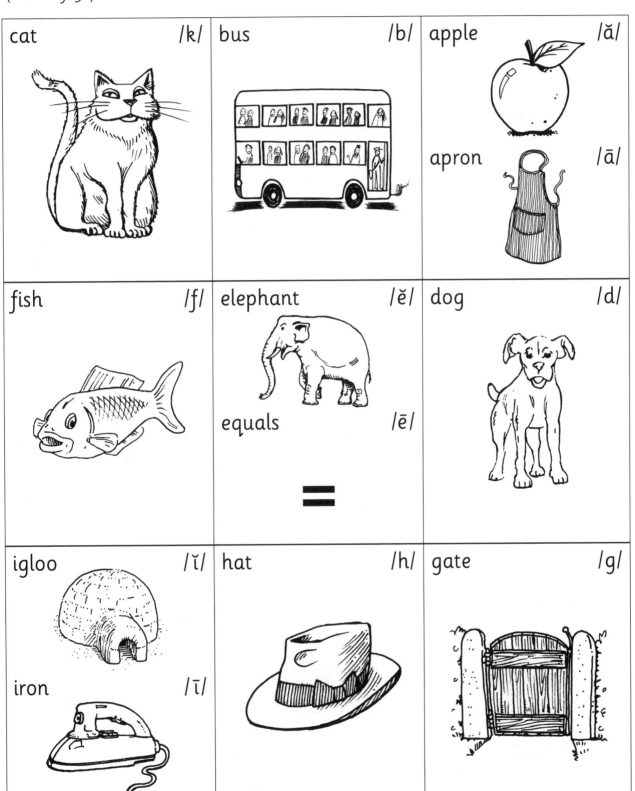

cat /k/	bus /b/	apple /ă/
		apron /ā/
fish /f/	elephant /ĕ/	dog /d/
	equals /ē/ =	
igloo /ĭ/	hat /h/	gate /g/
iron /ī/		

SECTION 5

Resource Sheet 5.6: **Back of Reading Pack cards B**
(Activity 91)

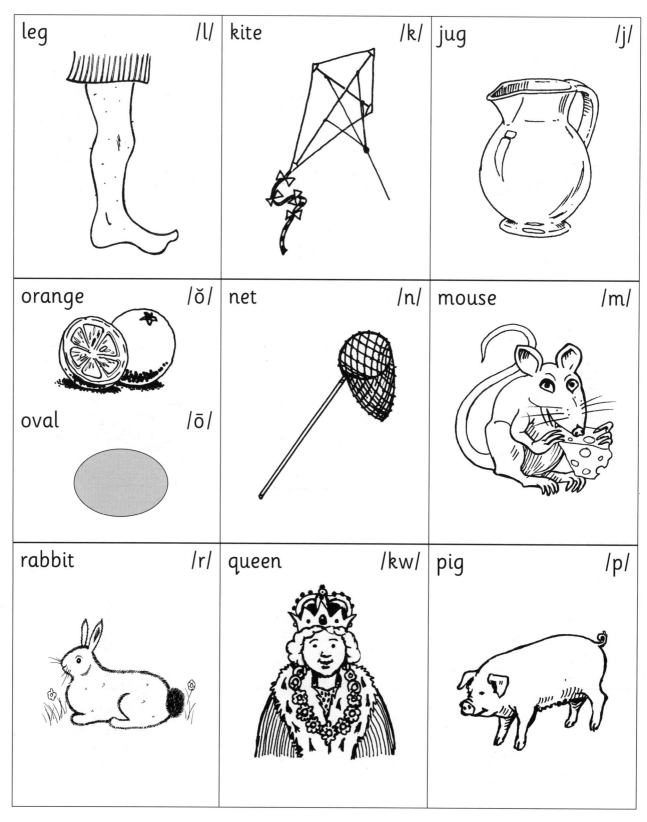

leg /l/	kite /k/	jug /j/
orange /ŏ/ oval /ō/	net /n/	mouse /m/
rabbit /r/	queen /kw/	pig /p/

Resource Sheet 5.7: **Back of Reading Pack cards C**
(Activity 91)

umbrella /ŭ/ unicorn /ū/	tap /t/	sun /s/
fox /ks/	window /w/	van /v/
	zip /z/	yo-yo /y/

Resource Sheet 5.8: **High-frequency words for children aged 4-5 years (Reception), 5-6 years (Year 1) and 6-7 years (Year 2)**

Ages 4–5 years (Reception)

I	at	are	am	big	in	it
up	for	this	cat	my	went	yes
look	he	going	to	mum	was	can
we	is	they	come	no	of	
like	said	away	day	dad	me	
and	go	play	the	all	she	
on	you	a	dog	get	see	

Ages 5–6 years (Years 1 and 2)

about	do	if	now	ran	then	way
after	don't	jump	off	saw	there	were
again	dig	just	old	school	these	what
an	door	last	once	seen	three	when
another	down	laugh	one	should	time	where
as	first	little	or	sister	too	who
back	from	live	our	so	took	will
ball	girl	lived	out	some	tree	with
be	good	love	over	take	two	would
because	got	made	people	than	us	your
bed	had	make	push	that	very	
beed	half	man	pull	their	want	
boy	has	many	put	them	water	
brother	have	may				
but	help	more				
by	her	much				
call	here	must				
called	him	name				
came	his	new				
can't	home	next				
could	house	night				
did	how	not				

> In addition, children are expected to learn to read:
>
> - the days of the week
> - the months of the year
> - numbers to twenty
> - common colour words
> - their name and address
> - the name and address of their school.

From the National Literacy Strategy *Framework for Teaching* Appendix List 1 (© Crown Copyright, October 1998). Reproduced with permission.

SECTION 6

Writing and handwriting

Introduction

Writing is a means of communicating the spoken word. Using correct spelling and being able to write using a legible, fluent script is a very important life skill. Pressures of time when working at school, university, in the workplace and elsewhere means that having a well-developed style of writing that is both legible and fast is very important – and this takes practice.

First steps

Most children begin to show an interest in writing between the ages of two and five years. Some children are keen to watch others write and then make their own marks on paper; others are not. It is important to foster a relaxed atmosphere in which children feel the marks that they make are valued. Therefore do not discourage children from writing by forcing them to sit and make letter shapes. Children often begin to write in role-play situations where they copy the things they observe adults doing – such as writing a shopping list, taking an order in a restaurant, or writing a birthday card. Opportunities for such play should be provided at home and in the nursery by making available a variety of different kinds of paper and writing utensils.

Formal teaching

Formal teaching of writing should begin once a child knows all the initial letter sounds and can form the symbols that represent them. This will ensure that once the child begins to write he can concentrate on the ideas and vocabulary rather than on the mechanics of forming the letters. A completely joined-up script will encourage the child to remember letter strings and patterns and will therefore help with accurate spelling. The use of lined paper is vital, and double lines are preferable at the early stages: a child needs the guidance of a line to keep his writing straight.

Pencil Grip

Children should be encouraged to adopt a 'tripod' or 'tripoint' pencil grip, with the pencil resting on the middle finger and the thumb and first finger gripping the pencil. To encourage this, a dot can be drawn on the first joint of the child's middle finger (this is the same for left- and right-handers) to show him where the pencil should rest. The tripod grip ensures that the writer has optimum flexibility of movement: he does not have to move his hand too much as he writes across the page. Some children learn an 'awkward grip', which is not a particular problem if they have neat handwriting, and it can sometimes be very difficult to change. However, the tripod grip should be encouraged in those who have not yet developed a grip and in those who struggle to keep their handwriting neat and legible.

Left-handed writers

Left-handed children should place their paper and turn their chairs to an angle facing right. This ensures they can see the top of their pencil, which must be kept sharp to enable the point to be seen, and will help to avoid the 'hook' position that many left-handers develop. A left-hander should never be seated next to a right-hander for a writing task as they will continually bump arms. A supplier of equipment for left-handed people is listed under 'Resources and Suppliers'.

Frequently asked questions

How do I teach a child to write his name?
At first there is nothing wrong with an adult writing a child's name on his paintings or other work. In fact, by modelling this you will be giving the child guidance as to how this is done. When the child first begins to form letter shapes alone, hold and guide his hand to discourage him from using incorrect letter formation. Incorrect letter formation tends to occur when children look at the letter shape and draw it from the visual clues. For example, the letter may resemble an 'a' but the child has gone around the circle twice and has drawn the stick far away from the main body of the letter. Tracing names is a good way of practising them, and eventually a child can learn to write his name by learning the dance your hand does in doing so.

Why is joined-up writing so important?

Handwriting is a motor movement, and letter shapes are held in your motor memory; this is the type of memory that makes possible touch typing, changing gear, playing the piano, and so on. As a competent writer, you can sign your name equally well with or without using your eyes (try it yourself!). Children need to be encouraged to have fluent letter formation in their motor memory so that they no longer have to think about letter shapes and can therefore concentrate on the spelling and content of their writing more readily. A completely joined script will encourage better spelling: common letter strings will be in the motor memory and this should lessen the chance of 'bizarre spelling', where children put down a random series of letters which do not form a recognisable word.

When should children start joined-up writing?

Encourage the child to start joining as soon as he learns to write; if a child starts to join from the beginning, his handwriting will soon become neat and legible. It is much harder to learn one style and then change to another because some of the bad habits will inevitably stick. Many schools and nurseries have adopted this methodology; however it is important to be sensitive to the handwriting style policy used in the setting the child attends.

Teaching guidelines

1 Model writing whenever possible.
2 Involve children in purposeful writing tasks, such as shopping lists or notes.
3 Encourage a correct pencil grip from an early age.
4 Handwriting patterns are an important precursor of a fluent joined script and children need many opportunities to practise this.

Remember

1 Do not rush the important stages of patterning and learning letter shapes.
2 Refer to letters by their names when forming them.
3 Be positive about any attempt at making marks that represent the written word.
4 Use the Writing and handwriting checklist (*Resource sheet 6.1*) to keep a record of the child's progress.

Developing fine motor skills

Activities for school and home

It is very important that children learn fine motor skills before formally learning to represent letter shapes as they will help the children to form a steady pencil grip.

Activity 92:
Fiddly fingers

Use your imagination to provide the children with plenty of games that require manual dexterity. For example, hide a bead in the centre of the playdough. Ask the child to pinch the dough in order to find the bead. Or ask the children to slowly tear up pieces of scrap paper, using two fingers. You can use the torn paper shapes later in a collage.

> **You will need:**
> threading beads, pegboards, playdough and scrap paper

Activity 93:
Finger rhymes and exercises

Place each finger tip so that it is touching the tip of your thumb (one hand at a time then both hands together). Stretch fingers wide and curl them to a fist. Encourage the children to do the same. There are many finger rhymes to try, for example:

Five little peas in a pea pod pressed
One grew, two grew and so did all the rest
They grew and they grew and they did not stop
Until one day the pod went pop!

As you recite this rhyme, clench your fingers into a fist then gradually release them to echo the meaning of the words; clap your hands loudly at the end.

SECTION 6

Here is the church, and here is the steeple
Look inside and here are the people.

With this rhyme start with your fingers locked together and palms down, point your index fingers together facing up to create a steeple, then turn your hands over to reveal the people inside the church.

Activity 94:

Maze puzzles

These are found in many puzzle books and pre-writing books and provide practice in drawing a pencil line between two other lines. Use copies of *Resource sheet 6.2* to give the child some further experience of pencil control.

Patterning

Patterning is a crucial precursor to handwriting. It encourages a sense of fluency in the hand and builds pencil control and an awareness of the space on the page. Patterns should be based on letter shapes but should not consist of recognisable letters (with the exception of the 'c' pattern).

Patterns should include:

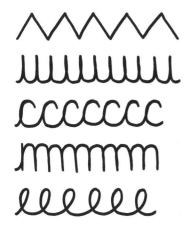

See *Resource sheets 6.3* to *6.5* for some examples.

Activities for school and home

Activity 95:
Movement ribbons

This activity is designed to develop gross motor skills. It involves drawing large patterns in the air with a length of wide ribbon attached to a small stick or pole.

You will need:
a pencil or small rod, with a length of wide ribbon tied to one end

Activity 96:
Finger patterns

Fill the tray with one of the materials listed below. Ask the children to use a finger to create a particular pattern. Choose from:

You will need:
a large long tray (a window box drip tray is ideal) and your choice from the materials listed below

- cornflour (mixed with a little water)
- flour
- rice or pulses (these need to be quite small to be effective)
- salt
- sand (wet or dry)
- sawdust
- sequins
- shaving foam
- soil
- sugar (icing or granules)

Alternatively you could ask the children to draw with one finger on a:

- carpet tile
- foam sheet
- tactile material such as velvet or Velcro®

Activity 97:
Patterning with chalks

- Chalk a large pattern on the ground for the children to walk or run along.
- Use chalk to draw patterns with the children, either on paper or on a paving slab or board.

You will need:
chalk, a large board or sheet of paper

Activity 98:
Patterning with paint

Here are some ideas for painting activities.

- Spread paint on a table or large tray, make a pattern with a finger or a stick, then place a piece of paper on top to make a printed image
- Paint with a wide variety of brushes, including sponge brushes
- Paint over pre-drawn patterns, or make the patterns freehand. Once dry, use a pencil torch to highlight the patterns by going over the pattern again with the beam
- Paint with water on a dry wall or outside surface.

Activity 99:
Patterning with pencils and pens

Children can trace over patterns before moving onto freehand work and the Resource sheets supplied will give them patterns practice. Using a variety of pencils and pens is very important: pick those that flow well and investigate using thick and thin barrels and nibs.

Activity 100:
Patterning with paper

- Use large rolls of paper (this can be used as backing for displaying other work)
- Cut out shapes such as hands (for mendhi patterns at Diwali), Christmas baubles, Easter eggs, elephants, leaves and so on, on which to make patterns
- Trace over pre-drawn pattern cards
- Use three colours, or three shades of one colour, to create effective patterns, such as shades of brown, yellow and orange on an autumn leaf.

SECTION 6

Handwriting

General activities for school and home

Eventually children need to be able to make their patterns small enough to draw between the lines of an exercise book; some children may not be ready for this until they are five years old or more. Once this is established – ideally in books with double lines, about 5mm apart at 12mm intervals – they can make a basic pattern keep within the lines in one continuous movement, then they are ready for the basic letter shapes.

Continuous cursive handwriting is a fluent style where every word starts from the line. Therefore all letters are introduced with an 'in' stroke. This eliminates the need to learn different starting points for each letter, as is the case with most other styles. The descenders have loops so that fluency is maintained; ascenders do not have loops. This means that the minority of children who have visual difficulties, and whose writing may flip over, can be sure which way up the writing should be.

Teaching letters

Letters should be introduced in groups based on a similar pattern and the names of the letters (rather than their sounds) should be used at all times. It is fine to say 'This is an 'i' and it can make the /ĭ/ sound', but the letter 'i' will eventually also make the sounds /ī/ /y/ /ē/. To avoid confusion in the future, it is best, therefore, to use letter names.

If you teach letter formation in the order suggested below, children will be able to base the letter shapes on patterns that they have practised:

'i l t u' (based on *uuuu* pattern) *i l t u*

'c a d g q s' (based on *ccccccc* pattern) *c a d g q s*

'n m h b p' (these letters begin with the 'stick') *n m h p b*

'o r v w' (these letters all join from the top) *o r v w*

'x z' (these are square letters) *x z*

'f j k y e' (these are the odd letters that do not follow a regular pattern). *f j k e*

As soon as each letter group has been introduced, ask the children to write or copy words comprising letters from that group. For example, from 'i l t u' you can make 'ill', 'lit', 'till' and 'tilt'. However, please remember that it is a handwriting exercise rather than a reading exercise.

Teaching handwriting

Start big, using carpet tiles, paint and large sheets of paper. Modelling is crucially important. As you model writing the letter, verbalise what you are doing so that you make this a multi-sensory activity. The child should copy with their finger the movements that you are making, whilst also verbalising. To start with, you might allow the child to trace over the letters you have drawn, to show them how the letter is formed. However, you must make sure that they are making the correct movements: as you walk around and check, keep verbalising the movement or hold the child's hand to guide his pencil. As the child becomes competent with the basic formation of the letter he can gradually make it smaller until he is able to trace or write it between the double lines of his exercise book. Eventually children will be able to copy your letters. However, you will need to check continually that letter formation is correct and that bad habits do not form.

Remember: only begin letter formation if you are sure that the child is ready for it. He should be able to form a fluent pattern in a controlled way, and the pattern should be consistent in size.

Photocopiable resource sheets for Section 6:
Writing and handwriting

- [ ] **6.1: Writing and handwriting checklist**

- [ ] **6.2: Maze**

- [ ] **6.3: Tracing sheet**

- [ ] **6.4: Pattern pictures**

- [ ] **6.5: More patterns to trace**

Resource Sheet 6.1: **Writing and handwriting checklist**

Name _____ Class _____

Date	Activity	Comments
19/11	Patterning	Produced a fluent zig zag pattern in tray filled with sequins (Activity 96)

SECTION 6

Resource Sheet 6.2: **Maze**
(Activity 94)

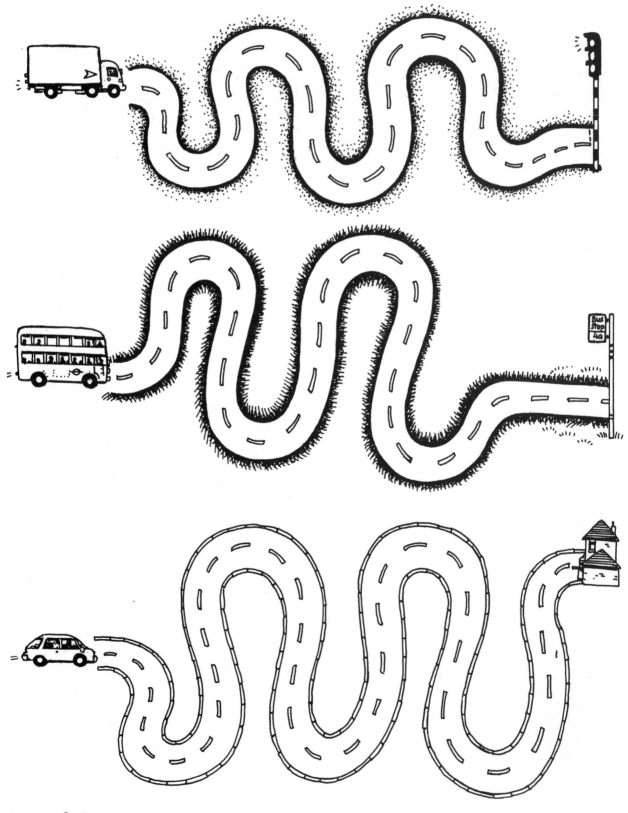

Resource Sheet 6.3: **Tracing sheet**
(Activity 99)

Resource Sheet 6.4: **Pattern pictures**
(Activity 99)

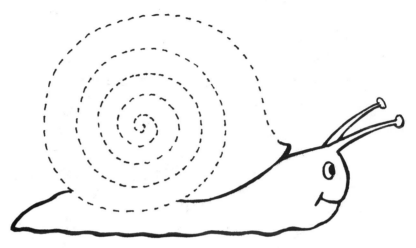

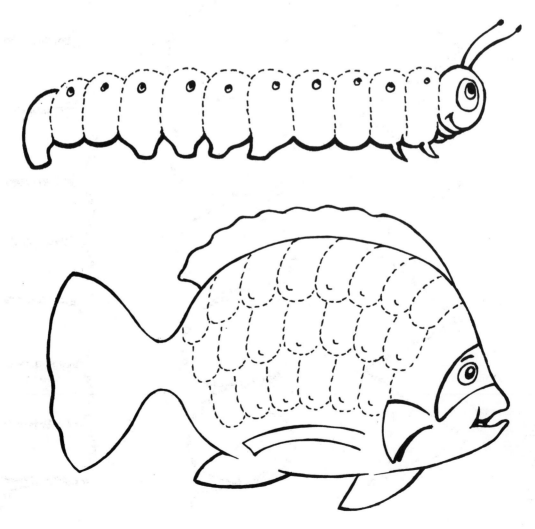

Resource Sheet 6.5: **More patterns to trace**
(Activity 99)

SECTION 6

Conclusion

By engaging in many of the activities within this book the child will have learnt the many skills that he needs if he is to develop into a skilled reader and writer whilst having fun. The child will have:

- An awareness of rhyme. Very helpful for both reading and spelling.
- Knowledge of the alphabet. Crucial for everyday tasks such as using a phone book or a dictionary.
- Phonological awareness. Without this a learner cannot tackle unknown words in reading or build up unknown words in spelling.
- Fluent reading and writing – the culmination of all their work on early literacy.

The methods and approaches used are designed to be as multi-sensory as possible, thereby engaging the learner through visual, auditory and kinaesthetic channels. This combination of approaches is successful for all children, especially those who may have dyslexic type difficulties. Its success lies in the fact that it engages every learner, regardless of his preferred learning style. Once the 'mechanics' of literacy are mastered, the child will have access to a fascinating world of information, and a lifetime in which to explore it.

Resources and suppliers

General items

Miscellaneous items that you will find useful include:

- sound lotto (Soundtracks games)
- coloured beads
- snap games
- cotton reels
- toy food
- rhyming pairs games
- shopping baskets
- chunky chalks

All of the above are available in good toy shops or toy departments, or through educational catalogues.

- Blindfolds can be made from pieces of material or old scarves. Some airlines provide them on long-haul flights.
- 'Feely bags' are simple cloth bags with a drawstring closure, as seen at craft shows. They are sometimes sold as shoe bags.
- Movement ribbons can be made from a piece of dowling with a length of thick ribbon attached. Gymnastic movement ribbons can be bought in sports shops with specialist gymnastic equipment or from physical education (PE) catalogues.
- Wooden alphabets. Many educational catalogues advertise these, including Galt and LDA: see www.galt.co.uk and www.ldalearning.com. They can also be purchased from:
    Cambridge House Dyslexia Resources
    Cambridge House
    10 Dry Hill Road
    Tonbridge
    Kent TN9 1LX
    Tel 01732 369822
    www.cambridgehouse-dyslexia.co.uk

Cards

- Sequencing picture cards
  Available in the ColorCards® series from:
  Speechmark Publishing Ltd
  www.speechmark.net

- Reading Pack cards
  Blank playing cards can be found in good stationers or in educational
  catalogues. Boxes of one hundred cards can be purchased from:
  Michele Bradbeer
  Tel 07885 984820
  e-mail: mbradbeer@hotmail.com

Stationery

- Berol Handhugger pens and pencils
  These triangular barrelled pens and pencils are available in many high
  street stationers and through educational catalogues. Thin triangular
  pencils are available from LDA:
  LDA Learning
  Abbeygate House
  East Road
  Cambridge CB1 1DB
  Tel 0845 120 4776
  www.ldalearning.com

- Join-the-dots books and mazes
  Good stationers stock a range of puzzle books for young children and
  some dot-to-dot alphabet books. Mazes can also be found in early
  writing skills books.
  A range of mazes and dot-to-dot books is available through:
  Byeway Books
  Appledram Barns
  Birdham Road
  Chichester
  West Sussex PO20 7EQ
  Tel 01243 531660
  www.autumnpublishing.co.uk

- Double lined exercise books
  There are various types of double lined books, but those recommended
  contain double lines 5mm apart at 12mm intervals.
  Available from:
    Philip and Tacey Ltd
    North Way
    Andover
    Hants SP10 5BA
    Tel 01264 332171
    www.philipandtacey.co.uk

Books, music, videos and DVDs

- Dyslexia Friendly Schools booklet and video
  Continuous Cursive Writing and How to Teach It booklet and video
  Available from:
    Oldfield Primary School
    Chiltern Road
    Maidenhead
    Berkshire SL6 1XA
    Tel 01628 621750
    www.oldfield.windsor-maidenhead.sch.uk

- **Jolly Phonics** (A comprehensive system of learning synthetic phonics)

  United Kingdom
    Jolly Learning Ltd
    Tailours House
    High Road
    Chigwell
    Essex IG7 6DL
    Tel 020 8501 0405
    e-mail: info@jollylearning.co.uk
    www.jollylearning.co.uk

  North America
    Jolly Learning Ltd
    50 Winter Sport Lane
    Williston
    VT 05495-0020
    Tel 1-800-488-2665
    e-mail: jolly.orders@aidcvt.com

- **Playing with sounds: A supplement to progression in phonics
  (ref: 0280-2004)**
    DfES Publications Centre
    PO Box 5050
    Annesley
    Nottingham NG15 0DJ
    Tel 0845 602260
    e-mail dfes@prolog.uk.com
    www.standards.dfes.gov.uk

● **Music for 'The Quartermaster's Stores'**
 Ta-ra-ra Boom-de-ay: Songs for everyone (CD)
 A & C Black Publishers Ltd
 38 Soho Square
 London
 WID 3HB
 Tel 020 7758 0200
 www.acblack.com

Other suppliers

● Early Learning Centre
 Mail Order Dept
 South Marston Park
 Swindon SN3 4TJ
 www.elc.co.uk

● Anything Left-handed
 57 Brewer Street
 London W1F 9UL
 Tel 020 8770 3722
 www.anythingleft-handed.co.uk

Useful organisations

- **Afasic** (Advice on speech and language difficulties)
  2nd floor
  50-52 Great Sutton Street
  London EC1V 0DJ
  Tel 020 7490 9410
  e-mail: info@afasic.org.uk
  www.afasic.org.uk

- **British Dyslexia Association**
  98 London Road
  Reading RG1 5AU
  Helpline tel 0118 966 8271
  www.bda-dyslexia.org.uk

- **Dyslexia Institute**
  133 Gresham Road
  Staines
  Middlesex TW18 2AJ
  Tel 01784 463 851
  www.dyslexia-inst.org.uk

- **Dyspraxia Foundation**
  8 West Alley
  Hitchin
  Herts SG5 1EG
  Helpline tel 01462 454 986 (10 am to 1 pm Monday to Friday)
  www.dyspraxiafoundation.org.uk

- **Makaton Vocabulary Development Project**
  31 Firwood Drive
  Camberley
  Surrey GU15 3QD
  Tel 01276 61390
  e-mail mvdp@makaton.org
  www.makaton.org

- **The professional organisation of teachers of students with specific learning difficulties (PATOSS)**
  PO Box 10
  Evesham
  Worcs WR11 1ZW
  Tel 01386 712650
  www.patoss-dyslexia.org

Other useful websites

- ICT (extensive reviews and recommendations)
  www.teem.org.uk
  www.becta.org.uk
  www.dyslexic.com

- Literacy
  www.literacytrust.org.uk
  www.rif.org.uk
  www.earlyliterature.ecsd.net
  www.enchantedlearning.com
  www.syntheticphonics.com

- Literacy difficulties
  www.dyslexiaa2z.co.uk
  www.dyslexia.com

- Curriculum guidance for early years education and Foundation Stage information
  www.qca.org.uk
  www.standards.dfes.gov.uk
  www.ngfl.gov.uk

Recommended books for young children

This is not designed as a comprehensive list, but as an introduction to some popular authors through a selection of books – all of them suitable for young children aged up to five years.

Books available in the UK

Ahlberg A & Ahlberg J, 1997, *Peepo*, Viking Children's Books, London.

Alborough J, 2004, *Where's My Teddy?*, Walker Books Ltd, London.

Brown R, 1992, *A Dark Dark Tale*, Red Fox, London.

Browne E, 1995, *Handa's Surprise*, Walker Books Ltd, London.

Burningham J, 2002, *Mr Gumpy's Motor Car*, Red Fox, London.

Butterworth N, 1998, *Thud*, Collins Picture Lions, London.

Campbell R, 1997, *Dear Zoo*, Campbell Books, London.

Carle E, 2002, *The Very Hungry Caterpillar*, Puffin Books, London.

Chichester-Clark E, 2005, *I Love You, Blue Kangaroo*, Andersen Press, London.

Dr Seuss, 2003, *The Cat in the Hat*, HarperCollins Children's Books, London.

Dodd L, 2005, *Hairy MacLary*, Puffin Books, London.

Donaldson J, 1999, *The Gruffalo*, HarperCollins Children's Books, London.

Hayes S, 2001, *This is the Bear*, Walker Books Ltd, London.

Hill E, 1983, *Where's Spot?* Puffin Books, London.

Hutchins P, 1993, *Titch*, Atheneum Books for Young Readers, Simon and Schuster, New York, USA.

Inkpen M, 2006, *Kipper Story Collection*, Hodder Children's Books, London.

Inkpen M, 2006, *The Blue Balloon*, Hodder Children's Books, London.

Kerr J, 2006, *The Tiger who came to Tea*, HarperCollins Children's Books, London.

Martin B, 2003 *Brown Bear, Brown Bear, What do You See?*, MantraLingua Publishing, London.

Murphy J, 1995, *Whatever Next?*, Macmillan Children's Books, London.

Murphy J, 1998, *A Quiet Night In*, Walker Books Ltd, London.

Rosen M, 1993, *We're Going on a Bear Hunt*, Walker Books Ltd, London.

Umansky K & Chamberlain M, 1993, *Pass the Jam, Jim*, Red Fox, London.

Waddell M, 2006, *Owl Babies*, Walker Books Ltd, London.

Books available in the USA

Bingham C, 2004, *Tractor (Machines at Work)*, DK Publishing Inc, New York.

Carle E, 1994, *The Very Hungry Caterpillar*, Philomel Books, New York.

Dr Seuss, 1960, *One Fish, Two Fish, Red Fish, Blue Fish*, Random House Inc, New York.

Flack M, 1977, *The Story about Ping*, Puffin Books, New York.

McBratney M, 1996, *Guess How Much I love You?*, Candlewick Press, Cambridge, Mass.

Martin B, 1996, *Brown Bear, Brown Bear, What do you See?*, Henry Holt and Co, New York.

Munsch RN, 1980, *The Paper Bag Princess*, Annick Press, Toronto, Canada.

Rosen M, 2003, *We're Going on a Bear Hunt*, Aladdin Paperbacks, New York.

Sendak M, 1988, *Where the Wild Things Are*, HarperCollins, New York.

Please note that many of the books on the UK list are also available in the USA.

References and further reading

Briggs S, 1999, *Learning Can Be Fun!* Books 1-3, Egon Publishers Ltd, Baldock.

Department for Education and Skills, 1998, National Literacy Strategy *Framework for Teaching common high frequency words*, DfES, London.

Department for Education and Skills, 2004, *Playing with sounds: A supplement to progression in phonics*, DfES, London (downloadable from www.standards.dfes.gov.uk).

Hornsby B, 1999, *Before Alpha: Learning Games for the Under Fives*, Souvenir Press, London.

Hornsby B, Shear F & Pool J, 1999, *Alpha to Omega: The A-Z of Teaching Reading, Writing and Spelling*, Heinemann, Oxford.

Layton L, Deeny K & Upton G, 1999, *Sound Practice: Phonological Awareness in the Classroom*, David Fulton Publishers, London.

Lloyd S, 1992, *The Phonics Handbook (Jolly Phonics series)*, Jolly Learning Ltd, Chigwell.

Matterson E, 1991, *This Little Puffin ...*, Puffin Books, London.

Nash Wortham M & Hunt J, 1990, *Take Time: Movement Exercises for Parents, Teachers and Therapists of Children with Difficulties in Speaking, Reading, Writing and Spelling*, Robinswood Press, Stourbridge.

Ostler C, 1999, *A Parents' Survival Guide: Dyslexia*, Ammonite Books, Godalming.

Ott P, 1997, *How to Detect and Manage Dyslexia*, Heinemann, Oxford.

Rose J, 2006, Independent Review of the Teaching of Early Reading, Department for Education and Skills, London (download at www.standards.dfes.gov.uk/rosereview/finalreport).